JB JOSSEY-BASS™
A Wiley Brand

T0300910

Successful Capital Campaigns From Start to Finish

THIRD EDITION

Scott C. Stevenson, Editor

WILEY

978-1-118-69060-4   ISBN

978-1-118-70392-2   ISBN (online)

Successful Capital Campaigns:
From Start to Finish
— 3rd Edition

Published by

Stevenson, Inc.

P.O. Box 4528 • Sioux City, Iowa • 51104

Phone 712.239.3010 • Fax 712.239.2166

www.stevensoninc.com

PRE-CAMPAIGN

Chapter 1:   **Where It All Begins** 5

- Steps for Preparing a Capital Campaign
- Big Gifts Require Monumental Dreams
- Timeline Maps Key Campaign Activities
- First-ever Campaign? Give Yourself Some Planning Time
- Know What Causes Campaigns to Fail
- Must Have Ingredients for Strategic Planning
- Strategic Planning Procedures
- Help Current Donors Own Your Upcoming Campaign
- Checklist Ensures Groundwork for a Campaign is Laid
- How to Build Enthusiasm for Your Capital Campaign
- Characteristics of a Campaign-ready Board
- Unlock Your Board's Campaign Potential
- Too Few Prospects? Map Out Plan to Change That
- Identify and Promote an Entry Level Project
- Bad Economy? Consider a Smaller Capital Campaign
- Get the Jump on Competing Campaigns
- Regularly Review Your Top 100 Individual Prospects
- Partner for Visibility, Not Dollars
- Are You Ready for a Campaign?

Chapter 2:   **How Ready Are You.... Really?** 13

- Spell Out Responsibilities Before Hiring Counsel
- Nine Steps for Selecting Campaign Counsel
- Considerations for Selecting a Consultant
- Questions to Guide a Campaign Consultant Search
- Measure Your Shop's Strengths and Weaknesses
- Improve Your Shop, Boost Abilities to Raise Major Gifts, With Internal Development Audit
- Measure Your Campaign Preparedness
- Have You Measured Your Constituency's Gift Potential?
- Mine Your Existing Database for Major Donors, Prospects
- Comprehensive Wealth Sweep Jump-starts Major Giving
- Use Predictive Modeling to Find Potential Donors
- Methods for Assessing a Donor's Giving Potential
- Four Rules of Thumb for Estimating Major Prospects' Assets
- Form Measures Prospect's Ability, Likelihood to Give
- Ask the Right Questions in Major Gift Discovery Calls
- Case Statement Prep
- Case Statement Essentials
- Develop a Persuasive Case Statement
- How to Sell Your Vision to Donor Prospects
- Involve Constituents in Crafting Your Case Statement
- Six Ways to Make Your Case Statement More Compelling
- Why Conduct a Feasibility Study?
- Feasibility Study Is a Pre-campaign Must!
- How to Begin a Planning Study for a Major Capital Campaign
- Feasibility Study Should Include a Definitive Timeline
- Justify the Decision to Not Conduct Study

Chapter 3:   **Setting the Size, Scope and Campaign Duration** 29

- Understand the Science of Determining Funding Priorities
- Look to Current Donors When Setting a Campaign Goal
- Prioritize Funding Projects Before Launching a Campaign

- *Anticipate Sources of Campaign Gifts Up Front*
- *Begin by Plugging in Prospect Names*
- *Scale-of-gifts Model Crucial for Success*
- *Create a Workable Campaign Pyramid in Seconds*
- *Can Your Board Fund a Third of Your Campaign Goal?*
- *Incorporate Planned Giving Into Capital Campaigns*
- *Endowment Vs. Capital Campaigns: Why the Difference Matters*
- *Pre-campaign Tip*
- *Assign Target Dates for Generated Gift Revenue*
- *Give Thought to Your Campaign Slogan*

Chapter 4:   **Bringing Structure and Organization to Your Effort** 36

- *The Board's Role Will Impact Campaign Success*
- *Share Expectations With Your Campaign Chair*
- *Campaign Leadership: Why Have Honorary Chairs?*
- *Why an Honorary Campaign Committee Makes Good Sense*
- *Consider Campaign Co-chairs*
- *Advice on Enlisting Campaign Leadership*
- *How to Train Your Campaign's Volunteer Leaders*
- *Keep Your Steering Committee Motivated*
- *Strengthen Board Member Solicitation Skills*
- *Solicitation Team Should Be Prepared*
- *Hold a Brief Meeting for Your Solicitation Team*
- *Weekly Reports Keep Committee Members Engaged, Motivated*
- *Time Foundation Proposals*

Chapter 5:   **The Quiet (Lead Gift) Phase** 42

- *Structure Your Campaign Phase to Maximize Quiet Phase Fundraising*
- *One Board Member Needs to Set the Precedent*
- *Factors That Impact Campaign Success*
- *Develop Solicitation Strategies for Top Prospects*
- *Scale of Gifts Helps During Closing Process*
- *Anatomy of a Major Lead Gift*
- *Encourage Restricted Gifts to Supercharge Your Fundraising*
- *Promote the Triple Gift in Capital Campaigns*

CAMPAIGN

Chapter 6:   **Publicly Announcing Your Campaign ... With Enthusiasm** 46

- *Plan the Public Campaign Phase Early*
- *Create a Campaign Announcement Checklist*
- *Campaign Kick-off Event Offers Chance to Highlight Major Gift*
- *Make the Most of Your Campaign Announcement*
- *Announce a New Gift as You Go Public With Capital Campaign*
- *Use a Challenge to Launch Your Major Capital Campaign*
- *Online Campaign Launch Reaches Broad Audience*

Chapter 7:   **Communications Crucial to Maintaining Momentum** 50

- *Creatively Share Campaign Progress Updates*
- *Items to Include on Your Capital Campaign Website*
- *Aid Campaign Solicitations With Architectural Renderings*
- *Capital Campaigns, Major Gifts and the Role of Social Media*
- *Foundation Challenge Gifts Help Carry Momentum*
- *How to Get Permission to Publicize Major Gifts*
- *Allow Donors to Share in Accomplishments*
- *PhotoBooth Project Enhances Capital Campaign, Much More*

- *Periodic 'Scale of Giving' Report Helps Visualize Progress*
- *Challenge Takes Advantage of Capital Campaign Momentum*

POST-CAMPAIGN

Chapter 8:   **Bringing the Campaign to a Successful Close** 56
- *Ideas for Maintaining Capital Campaign Momentum*
- *Reinvigorate the Later Stages of a Long Campaign*
- *Five Ways to Jump-start Stalled Campaigns*
- *Post-campaign Priorities*
- *No Campaign End Date? No Problem*
- *Gift Acknowledgement Protocols Reduce Confusion, Lessen Mistakes*
- *Create a Schedule of Pledge Redemption Reminders*
- *Monitor Campaign Pledge Payments Carefully*
- *Hard Work, Creativity Combine to Meet Challenge Grant Requirements*
- *Include Donors in Post-campaign Success*
- *Decide on Donor Recognition Prior to Capital Campaign*
- *Identify Ways to Demonstrate Gratitude*
- *Mark Construction Milestone With Topping-off Ceremony*
- *Consider Outdoor Billboards in Special Instances*
- *Avoid the Love 'em and Leave 'em Tendency*
- *Stewardship Tip*
- *Create Policy for Publicizing Momentous Gifts*
- *Campaign Evaluation Requires More Than Whether the Goal Was Met*
- *Campaign Ending? Forget the Gala*

Chapter 9:   **Capital Campaign Case Studies** 65
- *How to Get Your First Capital Campaign Off the Ground*
- *Reach Out to Supportive Families With a Children's Wall*
- *Set Goals to Exceed Feasibility Study Expectations*
- *Despite Economic Downturn, Campaign Transcends Boundaries*
- *College Conducts Successful Two-phase Campaign*

Successful Capital Campaigns: From Start to Finish, Third Edition.
Edited by Scott C. Stevenson.
© 2012 Stevenson, Inc. Published 2012 by Stevenson, Inc.

Successful Capital Campaigns: From Start to Finish — 3rd Edition

Where It All Begins

Any successful capital campaign is generally an outgrowth of the organization's strategic plan. The strategic plan legitimizes the campaign and the campaign makes realization of the strategic plan possible. Successful campaigns are also the result of collective dreaming that's grounded in reality. But before any nonprofit gets too far along in its dreaming, it's critical that all stakeholders — development staff, the CEO and top management, the board, top prospects and volunteers — establish ownership in what's about to unfold. Without that solid ownership, the effort may be doomed.

Steps for Preparing for a Capital Campaign

Capital campaigns are affected by many factors beyond the control of an advancement or development department. But the success of many campaigns rests just as much on the quality of preparation done before the campaign, says Jerry Smith, president and CEO of the J.F. Smith Group (Auburn, AL), an organization which has managed numerous nonprofit campaigns.

Here Smith offers some of the steps he has found indispensable in the process of launching a successful capital campaign.

- **Develop a strategic plan.** "This is the dreaming part of the process," says Smith. "If money were no issue, what would be your ideal vision? What would your facilities, programs, staff and infrastructure look like? Answering these questions can take several months, but it's important, because the resulting vision is what lead donors will respond to."
- **Define projects.** "Once you have a vision, you consider what projects can help realize it. When determining these projects, you want to give consideration to programs with the broadest immediate impact, programs donors will support, and programs that set the stage for subsequent campaigns. And while you don't need exact dollar amounts for each project, you do need to have a rough idea of how much various options will cost."
- **Select appropriate counsel.** "Our experience has shown that campaigns that don't use some kind of counsel succeed about 50 percent of the time, where those that do, succeed 80 to 90 percent of the time."
- **Prepare your infrastructure** (see sidebar). "Before you take steps outside your organization, you need to make sure

---

Preparing Internally for a Campaign

Jerry Smith, president and CEO of J.F. Smith Group (Auburn, AL) emphasizes internal preparation for capital campaigns. In particular, he advises:

- Developing policies and procedures for basic questions such as how to count deferred gifts or gifts-in-kind, how to record matching gifts, and how to receipt gifts uniformly and efficiently.
- Reviewing your donor database, including mechanisms for donor tracking, gift entry, pledge reminders, and stewardship procedures.
- Developing committees in key areas that will help guide, organize and execute gift acquisition strategies.
- Forming an internal advisory committee that will assist in the identification of prospective donors and devise effective ways to seek their support.

---

you have all the policies, procedures and internal structures needed to support a campaign."
- **Conduct a feasibility study.** "This is where you test the projects that came out of the strategic planning phase. You talk to key supporters to see what they think positives and negatives of the campaign might be. Feasibility study meetings are also a great cultivation tool."
- **Launch the campaign!**

Source: Jerry Smith, President and CEO, J.F. Smith Group, Auburn, AL. E-mail: jerrysmith@jfsg.com

Big Gifts Require Monumental Dreams

As the well-known "Field of Dreams" movie line goes: "Build it and they will come." It's like that with giving, as well: "Dream it and they will make it a reality."

But to attract unprecedented levels of giving, donors need to visualize and buy into big dreams of what could be. If those dreams don't exist and aren't shared, how can you ever expect to attract significant gifts?

As you formulate strategic plans for your nonprofit, help participants avoid small thinking. Share examples similar organizations that have made huge accomplishments as the result of principal philanthropic investments.

Remember, it's much easier to scale back a dream that can't get the necessary funding than it is to expand a small dream that can be easily funded.

Timeline Maps Key Campaign Activities

If you're anticipating a major campaign, creating a timeline can help stakeholders visualize what needs to happen when. The example at right is not intended to reflect the schedule you should follow in planning a capital campaign, nor is it inclusive of every type of action you will want to take, but it does illustrate the sequence of events you might incorporate throughout each campaign phase: planning; quiet; public; and post-campaign.

Anticipate that during the quiet phase — that period when you will be soliciting your most financially capable prospects — at least 50 to 60 percent of your campaign goal should be realized in gifts and pledges. Know, too, that as much as 95 percent of your campaign goal may come from this group that may comprise 5 percent of your constituency.

Content not available in this edition

First-ever Campaign? Give Yourself Some Planning Time

If your nonprofit has never conducted a capital campaign before, be sure to give yourself enough planning time to ensure a successful effort.

If, for example, you have three years to gear up for a capital campaign, your preparation outline might include:

Year 1
- Initiate new and build on existing relationships with those who can make commitments of $10,000 or more.
- Enlist financially capable and widely respected individuals to join your board.
- Complete a five-year strategic plan that involves your board and most capable and probable donors.

Year 2
- Continue to cultivate relationships with top 100 prospects.
- Secure competent fundraising counsel to assist in pre-campaign planning.
- Conduct a development audit to determine campaign preparedness, then implement recommendations.
- Develop a case statement based on the strategic plan and top funding opportunities.

Year 3
- Continue to cultivate relationships with capable prospects.
- Conduct a feasibility study with counsel assistance.
- Solicit board members for exemplary campaign commitments.
- Initiate the quiet (lead gift) phase of campaign.

Know What Causes Campaigns To Fail

If you can anticipate the potential pitfalls of capital campaigns, you can take steps to avoid them. Here are some common reasons why capital campaigns fail:

1. Absence of a financially capable board.
2. Insufficient numbers of prospects capable of making five-figure-and-above gifts.
3. Noncompelling funding projects.
4. Lack of ownership on the part of board members and would-be donors.
5. Insufficient planning (e.g., strategic plan, case statement, feasibility study).
6. Absence of a capable consultant.
7. Too much emphasis on many smaller gifts as opposed to focusing on the few who could account for 90 percent of the campaign goal.
8. Lack of staff training and internal preparedness (e.g., budget resources, personnel, database resources).
9. External factors (e.g., economy, competition with other philanthropic endeavors).

Must-have Ingredients for Strategic Planning

Strategic planning is critical to long-term success, but many organizations confuse it with either annual planning or long-range planning, says Michel Hudson, chief strategist at 501(c)onsulting (Round Rock, TX).

"Strategic planning is a directed effort to shape and guide what an organization is, what it does and why it does it — with a focus on the future," says Hudson. "It uses strategies to define a course of action but remains consciously responsive to changing environmental conditions."

Hudson says effective planning varies in style and approach, but generally incorporates several core ingredients, including:

- A mission statement that defines an organization's purpose, values, constituency and services, in one to three precisely worded sentences.

- A vision statement that provides an image of what success would look like for the organization. "The vision is your dream for the future," says Hudson. "It frames any proposed course of action."

- Pre-planning fact-finding such as conducting internal and external surveys and gathering organizational charts, past strategic plans and collateral materials (e.g., newsletters, brochures).

- Buy-in from all stakeholders, including both internal personnel and external supporters like top donors and supporters. "You can devise a great plan, but if you don't have the support needed to implement it, you've wasted your time," says Hudson.

- An off-site retreat for leadership-level collaboration and planning. "Usually you have a daylong retreat somewhere pleasant and peaceful, because you're going to be addressing difficult issues," says Hudson. To facilitate planning, she says the venue should be comfortable and have plenty of room, ways to record brainstorming (flip charts, etc.), wireless access and a sufficient number of power outlets. (She also recommends plenty of funding for lunch and snacks.)

- An outside facilitator to help run the meeting. "A consultant (paid or not) can bring an objective viewpoint to the process, and there is a real skill to facilitation — in being able to accomplish what you need without hurt feelings or political agendas."

- Follow-up undertaken by a designated task manager whose role is to assign strategic objectives to particular people with deadlines, collect data and chart progress.

Finally, Hudson suggests an annual review of the strategic plan. "Enough can happen in a year that you may need to revise your plan. A full planning session should only be necessary every two to three years, though."

Source: Michel Hudson, Chief Strategist, 501(c)onsulting, Round Rock, TX. E-mail: mhudson@501consulting.com

How to Prepare for A Planning Retreat

The limited duration of a strategic planning retreat makes careful preparation a must. Michel Hudson, chief strategist, 501(c)onsulting (Round Rock, TX), says organizational resources should be one of the first areas of attention. Critical questions include:

- **Personnel** — Who will be involved in planning discussions, both before the retreat and after it? What role will they play? Whom will you get to facilitate the retreat?

- **Budget** — How much funding is set aside for planning and executing ideas? Will it be enough to achieve the desired results?

- **Software** — What kind of reports can you generate from the software you have? Will you be able to track the information you need to make your plan work?

- **Data** — What data will you pull from your database and how will you analyze it? What data will you need to collect via surveys or focus groups?

- **Leadership** — Who will champion the plan. Who believes in it and is committed to making it work? How will this person be empowered and enabled?

Hudson says timing of a retreat can affect its success. "It can take several months to gather the collateral material, find the best time for the organization, conduct surveys and analyze the results, so you really need to allow enough time to make the process work," she says.

Strategic Planning Procedures

- Since not everyone can be invited to a strategic planning process, share a confidential summary of your meeting — stamped "draft" — with select prospects who were not in attendance and get their reactions to it before preparing the final document.

Help Current Donors Own Your Upcoming Campaign

It's a known fact that current annual donors are the best prospects for major campaign gifts. Their past gifts are a testament to their commitment. That's why it's so important to cultivate these valuable supporters toward the realization of major gifts even before the quiet phase of a capital campaign gets under way.

Help current contributors build ownership of your upcoming campaign by:

✓ Involving them in your strategic planning process and case statement preparation.

✓ Keeping them informed of items and issues that relate to future funding opportunities — through publications, direct mail and personal visits.

✓ Involving them in the life of your organization and its work as volunteers, board members, committee members, etc.

✓ Including as many constituents as possible in some aspect of your feasibility study.

✓ Conducting tours and putting donors in contact with both employees and those served by your organization.

Checklist Ensures Groundwork for a Campaign is Laid

In some ways, capital campaigns are risky enterprises, says Gail Perry, founder of Gail Perry Associates (Raleigh, NC). "You really, really don't want to fail. The memory of a failed or painfully drawn-out campaign can linger for decades and hurt you with both donors and the wider community."

To avoid such an experience, Perry advises thorough pre-campaign planning and preparation. And to help nonprofits do that planning, she developed a campaign checklist covering seven key areas: board members, volunteer leadership, donor prospects, development office infrastructure, case for support, institutional image and campaign timing.

"I've done numerous campaigns and even more feasibility studies, and when organizations undertake a capital campaign prematurely, these are the things we end up recommending," she says. "In some ways they're very simple, at the same time, they're absolutely critical. These are the steps fundraisers can take to stack the deck in their favor."

Perry says the issues her checklist covers generally require long-term attention, not quick fixes. "I have organizations that have been working on these steps for several years, building a body of quality prospects, staffing-up internally and building and educating their board. These are all efforts you should be undertaking anyway, but doing them with the specific goal of a campaign in the future brings a lot of focus to the process."

Three of Perry's seven checklist areas are pictured at right. The rest can be found on her blog at www.gailperry.com/2010/07/a-mistake-proof-capital-campaign-checklist.

Source: Gail Perry, Founder, Gail Perry Associates, Raleigh, NC. E-mail: gp@gailperry.com

Content not available in this edition

How to Build Enthusiasm for Your Capital Campaign

Of the many intangibles needed to make a capital campaign work, few are more important than enthusiasm. A campaign whose board members, staff and key supporters aren't fired up and ready to go is a campaign asking for trouble.

Schuyler Lehman, founder and CEO of Mission Advancement, a McKinney, TX-based fundraising consultancy, says the task of building enthusiasm needs to start early — very early.

"Institutional leaders need to engage their core group by casting a vision of the campaign from the very beginning — before engaging a consultant and before the feasibility study," he says. "Giving them the chance to see behind the curtain, to offer their feedback and suggestions when it really matters, is what gives them real ownership of the campaign."

Ownership is important because it goes hand-in-hand with enthusiasm, says Lehman. "Enthusiasm comes from awareness and education. Ownership comes from participation and planning. If people are pulled into early planning meetings and asked how they would shape a campaign, so it would be compelling to people like them, they will see their fingerprints on it, and will have both ownership and enthusiasm for it."

Some of the reasons campaigns lose momentum, or fail to start with it are beyond organizers' control. But others can be planned for. In preparing your campaign, Lehman says to make sure you have:

1. Close relationships with a central core of donors. "Solicitation is similar to proposing marriage; you should never do it unless you're fairly sure of getting a yes. And you shouldn't start a campaign unless you're fairly sure you can get a good number of yeses."
2. The engagement of top leaders in the organization.

"Occasionally, presidents and CEOs will say they're just not willing to play a large role in a capital campaign. That's a big red flag, because the campaign is immediately hampered. No surrogate can truly take the place of a top leader."

3. A history of good stewardship. "A reputation for not being a good steward of resources — things like mismanaging funds — inevitably dampens enthusiasm. If you're in that situation, it might be wise to take some time to rebuild public trust."

Source: Schuyler Lehman, Founder and CEO, Mission Advancement, McKinney, TX.
E-mail: Slehman@missionadvancement.com

Building Enthusiasm Through Themes and Gimmicks?

Are strategies like theme days or button badges an effective way to build campaign enthusiasm? They can play a role, says Schuyler Lehman, founder and CEO of Mission Advancement (McKinney, TX).

"I don't know how effective they are in getting donors to respond financially, but they do have value in making people feel like they are involved in something bigger than themselves. I sometimes encourage organizations to put up a billboard during a campaign, not because it will raise money, but because it will remind staff and volunteers of the project's place in the community."

Characteristics of a Campaign-ready Board

Knowing your board will play a critical role in your campaign's success, and getting members to recognize that, is a major accomplishment. So how will you know when they have "arrived"? What characteristics will manifest themselves among the campaign-ready board?

These are characteristics that describe a board committed to campaign success:

- ❑ Board members own your strategic plan, because they helped design it.
- ❑ They are prepared to make their own sacrificial leadership gifts first.
- ❑ Board members willingly attend campaign meetings and make solicitation calls.

- ❑ They have major gift solicitation experience.
- ❑ They recognize successful campaigns are elitist, not populist.
- ❑ The board includes one or more model members who give inspiration to others.
- ❑ They make realistic commitments of time and knowledge.
- ❑ They grasp the quiet phase strategy of a major campaign.
- ❑ They maintain momentum and enthusiasm throughout the campaign.
- ❑ They know that the bulk of support will come from individuals, not corporations.
- ❑ They are committed to the campaign and recruit others to help.

Unlock Your Board's Campaign Potential

Knowing board gifts can account for a third or more of a capital campaign goal, and recognizing that board support establishes the precedent for gifts to follow, what steps can and should you take to prepare board members for unprecedented campaign gifts?

Assuming you already have a board in place that includes financially capable trustees, here are some top recommendations from The Major Gifts Report's panel of experts for encouraging those board members to give at their full potential:

1. **Be sure board members are part of ongoing strategic planning process.** If they are to commit to an ambitious and successful campaign, they need to own the entire process that leads up it. Include them — collectively and individually — in designing a long-term plan for your organization. Help them understand the need for additional resources and what the realization of those resources can accomplish.

2. **Make board members aware of what other successful nonprofits have achieved.** To help raise the sights of your board, share examples of what other charities have accomplished with campaigns. The more examples they see, the more they will understand that they, too, can do the same.

3. **Include lofty goals in your pre-campaign vision.** If you think small, your board will do the same. Instead, everyone needs to reach for goals that will stretch them beyond what they believe they are capable of. Board members need to believe that the identified goals are critical and must be

achieved to adequately fulfill the organization's mission. You can always scale back goals if necessary, but it's nearly impossible to expand them once a strategic plan has been established.

4. **Cultivate key board members' attention prior to feasibility study.** A feasibility study's results — based on individual and group interviews that include board members — determine the final campaign goal. So it's important before your feasibility study to cultivate individual interest in the campaign with board members whose financial ability can set a precedent. Meet one-on-one to measure both interest in the campaign and in specific giving opportunities. Develop a sense of those persons' potential interests before the feasibility study. Convince them that the magnitude of an eventual campaign will be determined, in part, by the example they set.

5. **Approach board members sequentially based on both gift capability and inclination to give.** Once the feasibility study has been completed and a goal recommended to the full board, approach first those few board members whose sacrificial pledges will send a clear signal to others that this campaign is more significant than any previous effort in the organization's history.

Many facets of the pre-campaign phase are important. If your board members cannot become passionate about the effort and their individual responsibilities in making it a success, it might be best to rethink your plans.

Too Few Prospects? Map Out Plan to Change That

Far too many organizations launch a major fundraising effort without first evaluating whether they have enough capable prospects to get the job done. Then, once a campaign is announced, it becomes clear that they have too few friends capable of giving five-figure-and-above gifts.

If lack of major gift prospects is an issue for your organization, make it a top priority to develop a three- to five-year identification and cultivation plan. That way, when you ultimately launch a major fundraising effort, you'll have a pool of capable and committed prospects.

The basic components of that three- to five-year plan should include:

1. Recruiting a board of trustees capable of making five-figure-plus gifts — perhaps a higher minimum depending

on your organization's stature and history. (Your board should set the example for all gifts that follow.)

2. Identifying your region's most financially capable individuals, businesses and foundations, which includes prioritizing this group based on research and rating and screening procedures.

3. Developing an ongoing plan of cultivation tailored to each prospect. As a guide, plan on a minimum of six highly individualized cultivation moves before embarking on the solicitation phase. This is in addition to more broad-based cultivation moves (e.g., inviting prospects to a reception).

4. Undertaking a strategic planning process that seeks to involve and engage these identified prospects in various capacities: planning, serving on advisory committees, completing perception surveys and more.

Identify and Promote an Entry Level Project

Looking for a way to enlarge your base of major gift donors? Come up with a $200,000 project that requires 20 gifts of $10,000 each.

If you're seeking gifts from non-donors who have the ability to make major gifts, get them on board by inviting them to make a modest investment in a compelling project, one that will energize them and result in an immediate positive impact for your organization and those you serve.

Begin by enlisting a handful of individuals willing to help spearhead the project, even help to select from among the funding opportunities you have in mind. Engaging a handful of individuals will help to energize them and motivate them to assist in identifying and approaching the remaining donors.

This spoon-feeding approach will help to build long-term relationships that will one day result in much larger gifts.

Bad Economy? Consider a Smaller Capital Campaign

If your organization is facing a difficult fundraising environment, a smaller, project-based capital campaign might be just what the doctor ordered.

"The basic motivation ... is the same in any size campaign. But smaller campaigns can be more easily planned and managed," says Janice Davis, CEO and executive director of the Ronald McDonald House Charities of Tampa Bay (FL).

Davis has first-hand experience with efforts of this kind. The ongoing Room For Change campaign, launched in January 2011 to help refurbish the Tampa House, is one of the nonprofit's smallest-ever campaigns, at $250,000. It has raised about $100,000 to date and received gifts ranging from $2,000 to $25,000.

Small campaigns support many of the year-end goals nonprofits normally pursue, but provide more visibility and recognition opportunities, she says. Project campaigns also help attract corporate support.

Davis says smaller campaigns use some, but not all, of the tools associated with larger ones. The Room For Change campaign, for example, included a large communications push and case statement, but went without a campaign director, feasibility study, silent/public phase structure and extensive prospecting. "In a campaign this size, you know who your major donors are, and you focus on making your case to them and the community."

But effective as they can be, smaller campaigns also present some unique challenges. "Visibility can get crowded, and competition from bigger campaigns sometimes overshadows smaller ones," says Davis. "New campaigns are rolling out every day, and there is always competition for attention and interest."

Source: Janice Davis, CEO and Executive Director, Ronald McDonald House Charities of Tampa Bay, Tampa, FL. E-mail: jdprmh@tampabay.rr.com

Get the Jump on Competing Campaigns

Although there may be a right time for your specific capital campaign, chances are yours will always be competing with other local and regional efforts. Some communities attempt to limit the number of campaigns going on at any one time, but even that can be difficult, as many worthwhile nonprofits compete for donor dollars.

Knowing your organization will be competing for limited philanthropic resources, what can you do to ensure your cause is getting the full attention it deserves from potential funders?

Here are four absolutes:

1. **Be sure your heaviest hitters know you plan to approach them for support.** Even if your campaign is in the quiet stage, make your lead prospects aware of your campaign and your intent to solicit them in the not-too-distant future.

2. **Approach your prospects with projects that will appeal to them.** If potential funders have no favorite charities, they will either select one or two or divide their philanthropic dollars equally among all who approach them.

If, however, you can present a fund opportunity that they find particularly appealing, the likelihood of more generous funding will increase significantly.

3. **Send in your biggest guns.** Match prospects with board and volunteer solicitors whose stature demands a significant pledge. It's much easier for a prospect to say no to a development officer than to a friend or business associate in his/her same league.

4. **Help key audiences understand that yours is the campaign to support.** Get board members and other insiders to help set the tone for your campaign. Some of this can be accomplished through one-on-one conversations and more can be accomplished in group social settings. The number and types of strategies you set forth will determine the level of community enthusiasm for your campaign.

Employ these steps to help your capital campaign stand apart and above others in the crowded, competitive field of nonprofit fundraising.

Regularly Review Your Top 100 Individual Prospects

Your top 100 prospects represent a dynamic, ever-changing group of individuals.

To properly rank and steward this important group, review your list regularly — at least monthly — and prioritize who should remain, who should be added and who should be moved to a lower priority (or inactive) level.

Include in this review process criteria related to both capability and inclination to give.

Give staff and highly involved board members a list of your current top prospects, along with additional names not presently on that list. Instruct those persons to first review the list individually, assigning a rating of 1, 2 or 3 beside each prospect's name — 1 meaning keep on the list, 2 meaning discuss for possible change in status, and 3 meaning recommendation to add to the list.

Then, meet as a group to compare your thoughts and adjust your top 100 prospect list accordingly.

Partner for Visibility, Not Dollars

What advice would you give to an organization undertaking a first capital campaign?

"Smaller organizations often have a somewhat tepid brand. They might be doing great work, but they're not that visible, and they don't have much name recognition. For a place like that, I would suggest partnering with a larger agency that could more effectively raise awareness of the campaign. The goal in that situation is not so much to secure sponsorship, but visibility. Your initiative has a much better chance of succeeding with that exposure than it would without it."

Source: Janice Davis, CEO and Executive Director, Ronald McDonald House Charities of Tampa Bay, Tampa, FL. E-mail: jdprmh@tampabay.rr.com

Are You Ready for a Campaign?

Ask around. You'll probably come to the same conclusion. Most capital campaigns fail due to a lack of planning up front. Whether campaigns are a way of life or a new challenge to your nonprofit, it's wise to ask yourself some pointed questions up front, prior to a feasibility study, to determine your organization's preparedness for a capital campaign.

Direct answers to these questions will help to determine your campaign readiness:

- ☐ **How genuine are our campaign needs?** You may think you need a new parking ramp, but how willing is your constituency to support such an effort? It's vital that fulfillment of campaign needs takes into account their "fundability." In other words, is it the kind of project that donors would find appealing to the point of contributing major gifts? Will completion of the project make a noticeable difference in your nonprofit's ability to fulfill its mission? Will those you serve notice a difference and be better served?

- ☐ **Do we have a constituency base that is able and willing to respond to those needs?** Have you had a capital campaign in recent years? If so, who were the major donors? These past contributors will be your most likely supporters for a new campaign. If you have not held a major campaign, it is important to evaluate your current donors' giving history. How many gifts have you received at various levels on an annual basis? Rate existing prospects. How large is your mailing list, and how familiar are your community or constituency with your organization?

- ☐ **Do we have the resources needed to adequately carry out campaign objectives?** If your constituency is scattered geographically, do you have the available resources to make personal visits to prospects? Do you have sufficient numbers of staff? What about your computer hardware and software — is it adequate to accommodate the requirements of your campaign? It sometimes pays to consider a campaign audit conducted by a consultant to determine your internal preparedness for a campaign. An outsider can often convince the CEO of development needs (e.g., additional fundraising personnel, upgraded equipment, etc.), that otherwise never seem to be funded.

- ☐ **How committed is our board to achieving campaign success?** If you've done your homework, it's not uncommon for board gifts to account for as much as 30 to 60 percent of your campaign goal. Board members need to be more than convinced of the need for a capital campaign. They need to make commitments that will set the pace for gifts that follow. Board members also need to be willing to identify and solicit other major gifts, if the campaign is to be successful.

- ☐ **How competent and prepared is our staff?** Who among the fundraising staff has previously been involved with a capital campaign? Those nonprofits with little or no background in capital campaigns would be wise to consider a consultant both in the preparation phase and throughout the campaign's duration. Once again, a campaign audit conducted by outside counsel will help to determine staff competency and the potential need for additional staff.

If these questions have been fully addressed, and you're still prepared to initiate a capital campaign, a feasibility study will help determine a realistic, yet challenging goal, as well as the campaign format and its duration.

Successful Capital Campaigns: From Start to Finish — 3rd Edition

PRE-CAMPAIGN

How Ready Are You.... Really?

Although many may point to campaigns that achieved their goals without the aid of philanthropic counsel, most turn to consultants to ensure the right steps are being taken from beginning to end. A successful capital campaign is much more than making goal. It's about building ownership in the effort; it's about identifying the best funding opportunities; it's about internal preparation and goal setting procedures and much more. An experienced consultant brings an orderly flow to the process and ensures that no step in that process is ignored.

Spell Out Responsibilities Before Hiring Counsel

Whenever you hire fundraising counsel, be sure to clarify the firm's role, in writing, at the onset, to minimally include:

1. What the firm will do for your organization. Describe various functions separately: internal audit, feasibility study, case statement development, etc.

2. Names of persons from the firm who will be responsible for specific roles: Who will be responsible for various aspects? Who will be the primary contact? Who will make regular visits to your organization and/or with prospects or donors? Who will be responsible for making reports to you and your board?

3. What is the timeline for consultant involvement? In addition to an overall timeline, each component of the consultant's responsibilities should include deadlines.

4. Detailed fees and expenses. Some consultants have flat per diem rates while others charge according to type of job. Some even have different rates based on size of organization for which they are working. Most charge separately for expense reimbursement.

5. An opt-out option. Any written agreement should allow you to discontinue work with the consultant if you choose: "This agreement may be cancelled upon 30 days written notice by either party."

Nine Steps for Selecting Campaign Counsel

"Everyone wants to be a consultant, and anyone who has conducted a successful capital campaign will tell you they're a fundraising consultant. But it's up to you to make sure they can actually help your organization," says Jerry Smith, president and CEO of the J.F. Smith Group (Auburn, AL), a fundraising consultancy with over 20 years of experience.

Smith shares a nine-step process he has developed for finding the campaign counsel best suited to your organization's needs and capacities.

1. **Talk to your peers** and create a list of possible fundraising advisors.

2. **Research those firms' websites** with an eye toward answering questions like: With what kind of organizations do they work? What are their track records? How long have they been in business?

3. **Create a list of your top five or six candidates** and conduct initial phone interviews to narrow the list down to three.

4. **Select a committee to conduct the interviews.** This committee should offer impressions and advice, but a senior leader such as a vice president of institutional advancement should make the actual recommendation.

5. **Create a list of questions for references** and have each committee member call three or four. Questions could include: Would you hire this firm again? How often did you meet the principle of the company? Did your campaign meet its timeline? What was cost per dollar raised?

6. **Narrow your list down to two companies** to invite for more in-depth, in-person, on-site interviews. Smith advises against inviting more than two and suggests that both companies be interviewed consecutively on the same day, with a half-hour break in-between to debrief.

7. **Standardize the interview process** by asking the same questions of both companies.

8. **Make sure the company brings key personnel,** such as the person who will be assigned to the campaign and the person who will do the feasibility interviewing, to the interview.

9. **Take the company representative(s) to lunch or dinner** following the interview. This allows you to ask any questions that were omitted during the initial interview and get a better feel for the style and personality of each. (Representatives of each company should be taken out separately.)

Source: Jerry Smith, President and CEO, J.F. Smith Group, Auburn, AL. E-mail: jerrysmith@jfsg.com

Considerations for Selecting a Consultant

If your nonprofit is considering hiring a campaign consultant, answer these questions to help narrow your list of qualified candidates:

1. **Experience** — How long has the firm been in business? How many campaigns has it managed? Have the firm's representatives dealt with campaigns for organizations similar to yours? Have they helped plan campaigns of the size and scope you are considering?

2. **Staff** — Are consultants full-time employees of the firm or is work subcontracted to others? What is the background of the firm's staff? Do they have experience running campaigns such as yours? Do they have a large enough staff with the experience you will need? Does their style of working match well with your organization and your constituents? Who will be assigned to your campaign, and what level of experience do they possess?

3. **Location** — Is this a national firm with several regional offices? Is one region more specialized than others? Does the firm have an office near you? Are they familiar with the territory and its economic influences?

4. **Cost** — How do their costs and the services compare to those of other consultants? What is and is not included in their base rate? Can you select from a variety of levels of service and cost?

5. **References** — Can the firms offer references from recent campaigns, especially for nonprofits similar to yours? How do references rate the firm's services? What were the firm's strengths, weaknesses? Would they hire that firm again? Why or why not?

> ### Online Resources for Philanthropic Consultant Lists
>
> ✓ The Giving Institute — www.givinginstitute.org
>
> ✓ Association of Fundraising Professionals — www.afpnet.org
>
> ✓ Association for Healthcare Philanthropy — www.ahp.org
>
> ✓ Council for Advancement and Support of Education — www.case.org

Questions to Guide a Campaign Consultant Search

Given their impact on the planning, organization and execution of a capital campaign, it is no exaggeration to say that campaign consultants can make or break a major fundraising project. Choosing the right advisor, therefore, is a task that should not be overlooked.

The following questions, developed by the Illinois Facilities Fund (Chicago, IL), a nonprofit lender and consultant that helps other nonprofits finance, plan and build mission-critical facilities, provide a foundation for your selection committee to begin assessing candidates' qualifications and "fit" with your organization.

- How does the consultant approach working with clients — both board and staff? Ask the candidate to describe an example of how he or she has worked with board members, both individually and as a group, to achieve program goals.

- What experience does the consultant have with public relations, communication and marketing, and how does he/she see those efforts affecting fundraising in a capital campaign?

- How would the consultant integrate a capital campaign with existing corporate and foundation operating support efforts?

- What role has prospect research played in the consultant's past efforts?

- What strategy would the consultant recommend for launching the capital campaign?

- What factors does the consultant think contribute to achieving campaign goals quickly? Or can objectives be met quickly at all?

- How soon would the consultant develop a work plan? What would that plan include?

- What checkpoints would be set up as the consultant worked with staff and board members on implementation?

- How involved would the consultant be with various plan elements, such as prospect research? How much will be demanded of organization staff time?

- What are the natural links and divisions between tasks assigned to the consultant and staff? How would he/she involve staff in the campaign? What are some examples of the kinds of things staff will need to do?

- What board training will be included? How much time will be spent training and preparing the board?

- What specific challenges and opportunities does he/she see for your organization?

The full document from which these questions were taken can be found at www.iff.org/resources/content/4/0/documents/TA4.pdf.

Measure Your Shop's Strengths and Weaknesses

The best way to make improvements in our personal lives is to honestly assess our strengths and weaknesses and then make adjustments that will diminish the weaknesses and enhance our strengths.

A similar approach should be used in evaluating the effectiveness of your development operation. It's referred to as a development audit and serves as a valuable process in improving both short- and long-term fundraising success.

Many organizations employ the services of a consultant to perform a development audit. Others conduct regular self-audits. Both methods have their pros and cons.

Whether you choose to hire outside counsel or conduct your own development audit, here is a checklist of systems, programs and structures that should be analyzed to determine their effectiveness in the overall fundraising operation:

- **Qualifications of existing personnel.** What are the strengths and weaknesses of each member of the development team? Who has experience with capital campaigns? Who needs additional exposure to the basics of planned gifts? Identifying individuals' strengths and weaknesses is a first step in advancing the proficiency of your team.

- **Review of job descriptions and organizational structure.** Does everyone have a job description? Have they been updated to conform to current responsibilities of each team member? In addition, who reports to whom? Is there a better way of structuring the operation for effectiveness?

- **Budget review.** Are you using existing resources to maximize your fundraising performance? Do you have adequate resources to generate new and increased gifts? This is where consultants can often be more effective in pointing out the need for additional development dollars and personnel.

- **Gift history.** It's important to have a clear history of gift support as well as sources of support. How much has been raised on an annual basis? Were the funds restricted or unrestricted? How diversified is the funding base and how much did each constituency contribute? What were the largest gifts?

- **Adequacy of support systems.** How are files organized for maximum effectiveness? Are computer capabilities sufficient? How are gifts processed, tracked and acknowledged?

- **System of prospect identification, research, cultivation, solicitation and stewardship.** How are prospects tracked? What methods of prospect research are being utilized? Who is managing the major gift prospect pool, and how is it being managed? How many prospects exist? How

many past donors are there, and at what levels have they contributed?

- **Board strength and involvement.** What is the current makeup of the board? To what degree are board members involved, and how much do they contribute annually? Is it a "hands-on" or "rubber-stamp" board? To what degree have board members been trained?

- **Volunteer strength and involvement.** How many volunteers are involved with the organization and in what ways? To what degree are they structured? How significant is their current involvement in the life of the organization? Are they fully trained for their jobs?

- **Campaign preparedness.** When was the last campaign? How much was raised? How many contributors gave at which levels? How were the funds used? What was the role of board and volunteers in the effort?

- **Communications analysis.** What printed materials exist that support the development effort? How often is direct mail utilized throughout the course of a year? What does each appeal consist of, and how effective has it been? Have all team members been adequately trained in making presentations and solicitation calls?

- **Media and public relations.** How frequently do news releases appear and in which papers? Does the organization have a clear set of identity guidelines? Is the agency's presence clearly felt by the community or region? What "partnerships" exist between the organization and the community?

- **Operational plan analysis.** There should be a written plan detailing development plans for the year. Does it provide quantifiable goals and objectives with strategies on how to achieve each objective? Does it include an action plan and schedule of activities and events to take place?

- **Strategic plan analysis.** Does the organization have a long-range plan that addresses fundraising needs over a period of five years or more? How does it complement ongoing fundraising efforts? Does it include plans to generate endowment gifts?

- **Planned gifts review.** Does the agency have an active planned gifts program in place? Has the board adopted a planned gifts policy, and are members fully supportive of the planned gifts program? Does the program include quantifiable goals and objectives as part of the overall operational plan? How many prospects exist? How many expectancies are there, and what is the estimated amount in planned gift expectancies? How are prospects identified and cultivated?

How Ready Are You.... Really?

Improve Your Shop, Boost Abilities to Raise Major Gifts, With Internal Development Audit

Fundraising professionals are often intimidated by the thought of an internal development audit, but they needn't be, says Linda Lysakowski, president and CEO of the fundraising consultancy, Capital Venture (Las Vegas, NV).

"The purpose of development audits is to help you build on strengths and address the challenges you face, not point fingers or assign blame," says Lysakowski. Most development audits take financials as a key area of analysis. Lysakowski says organizations should focus on factors such as:

❑ How much revenue is being raised.

❑ Through what avenues the money is coming.

❑ How the organization's cost to raise a dollar compares with national averages.

❑ Ratio of grants received to grant requests made.

❑ What percentage of staff time and resources are being spent in what areas (annual fund, special events, grants, major gifts, etc.).

Effective development audits go beyond dollars to look at deeper structural issues, the fundraising consultant says, both within the development office and in the organization as a whole.

"You want to look at the governance structure, the involvement of board members, the staffing situation and the attitudes of other departments toward fundraising," she says. "You should also consider public relations and communications, as they can have a big impact on fundraising."

Lysakowski says development audits are often done in conjunction with fundraising milestones such as launching a capital campaign or developing a planned giving program — often as a way to justify proposals to skeptical or hesitant board members.

She says major audits are best conducted by outside consultants who can more effectively address delicate issues like board member participation and relationships between other departments and the development office than can internal staff. However, she also says nonprofits can and should conduct internal mini-audits on a regular basis.

To assist nonprofits in assessing their ability to succeed at raising funds, Lysakowski created a development audit tool. Shown, in part, at right, the tool provides a means for organizations to take a close look at their fundraising methods and strategies over the past year.

Source: Linda Lysakowski, President and CEO, Capital Venture, Las Vegas, NV.
E-mail: Linda@CVfundraising.com

Conduct an internal development audit using questions such as these, gleaned from a copyrighted audit created by Capital Venture (Las Vegas, NV).

Content not available in this edition

How Ready Are You.... Really?

Measure Your Campaign Preparedness

Just as it's possible to rate and screen major gift prospects, it is also possible to measure an organization's preparedness for a major campaign.

Those of you who have previously been involved with campaigns know a successful fundraising effort involves a great deal of planning time and preparation — in some cases, years.

Whether you are a seasoned professional or a newcomer to development, the campaign preparedness *scale* can provide one valuable measurement of an organization's readiness in launching a campaign.

The scale takes into account several factors that represent necessary ingredients for a successful campaign and assigns a weight to each of them. Their sum provides one way of analyzing an organization's ability to pursue major campaign gifts.

Here are descriptions of the first three factors included in the campaign preparedness scale:

- **Organization's age.** The longer your agency has been in existence, the better your odds of successfully implementing a major gift campaign. An organization's age reflects the time it has had to gain visibility and build a supportive constituency.

- **Percent of repeat contributions.** Of those on your mailing list, assuming you have a well-established list, what percentage contribute on an annual basis? If less than 25 percent contribute, for instance, you may have an inadequate pool of campaign prospects. Remember, past donors are among the best prospects for a campaign.

- **Years since last campaign ended.** Are you just completing a campaign, or has it been years since your institution embarked on a major fundraising effort? This is an important factor in determining an organization's preparedness for a campaign.

Content not available in this edition

How Ready Are You.... Really?

Have You Measured Your Constituency's Gift Potential?

Being able to estimate your constituency's gift potential at any given time plays a crucial role in planning for your organization's future and knowing how that future will be funded.

In order to determine your institution's overall gift potential, however, you must rate and screen those among your constituency. The process of rating and screening individuals, businesses and foundations will allow you to categorize prospects based on your estimates of their individual financial worth and giving potentials.

While there are varying rules of thumb for estimating giving ability, one such guideline states: If a prospect is well cultivated, highly motivated and effectively solicited, she/he could be expected to contribute 5 percent of annual income over a five-year period or 10 percent of the individual's net worth over the same period.

An individual with a $60,000 income would, for instance, be likely to contribute $3,000 (5 percent) over five years; and an individual with a net worth of $500,000 would be capable of donating $50,000 (10 percent) over a five-year period.

Once individuals' giving potentials have been determined and categorized, the next step is to determine how many prospects need to be identified in each financial category in order to achieve your desired funding goal.

Once again, we turn to a rule of thumb to measure the number of prospects that need to be cultivated and approached: During a campaign, it will generally take at least three qualified prospects for each single gift you hope to secure at each giving level.

Based on that principle, you can compare your existing number of prospects in each giving category with the number of prospects required to achieve your desired campaign goal.

This comprehensive process of rating and screening prospects and then projecting the number of additional prospects needed, will help determine what remains to be accomplished in order to reach the desired funding goal.

Gift Request To Be Given Over Time	Based On Minimum Income	Minimum Assets
$10,000	$50,000	$200,000
$25,000	$100,000	$500,000
$50,000	$250,000	$500,000
$100,000	$250,000	$1,000,000
$500,000	$500,000	$5,000,000
$1,000,000	$500,000	$10,000,000

Rule of Thumb #1: If the prospect is well cultivated, highly motivated and effectively solicited, she/he could be expected to contribute 5 percent of annual income over a five-year period or 10 percent of the individual's net worth over the same five-year period.

The table at left represents another method which can be used to measure an individual's gift potential. Unlike the above rule of thumb, it is not based on a consistent percentage of income or net worth. Please keep in mind, these are only guidelines. A number of additional factors, like past giving history, timing, the donor's ability to replace assets, etc. should be considered in addition to the donor's financial ability.

5 Year Capability	Existing Constituency	Cumulative Capability	Proposed Campaign Goal	Gifts Required	Total Prospects Needed (3:1 Ratio)	Prospect Balance Needed
$1,000,000+	2	$2,000,000	$2,000,000	2	6	4
$500,000-999,999	7	$3,500,000	$3,000,000	6	18	11
$250,000-499,999	12	$3,000,000	$3,000,000	9	27	15
$100,000-249,999	21	$2,100,000	$2,500,000	25	75	54
$50,000-99,999	47	$2,350,000	$2,500,000	50	150	103
$25,000-49,999	110	$2,750,000	$2,500,000	100	300	190
$10,000-24,999	182	$1,820,000	$2,000,000	200	600	418
$5,000-9,999	300	$1,500,000	$1,500,000	300	900	600
$1,000-4,999	1,750	$1,750,000	$1,000,000	1,000	3,000	1,250
Total	2,341	$20,770,000	$20,000,000	1,692	5,076	2,645

Sample Prospect Potential Report

Rule of Thumb #2:
During a campaign, it will generally take at least three qualified prospects for each single gift you hope to secure at each giving level.

Mine Your Existing Database for Major Donors, Prospects

Since the key to building a major donor program is creating and maintaining relationships, look first to your database of supporters for potential major gifts, says Sandra G. Ehrlich, director of fund development services at Zielinski Companies (St. Louis, MO).

According to industry statistics, approximately 4 to 5 percent of the current donors in your database have the ability to make a major gift, says Ehrlich. For example, if your database contains 5,000 names, it should contain 150 to 200 potential major donors.

"Use your database to determine how many individuals are giving at a significant level," she says. "Begin by running a report of donors who have made a $1,000 single gift. If you find 10,000 donors, you'll need to revise your criteria. If you find 100, you are in the ballpark. If you find only two, drop the baseline to $500 and go from there."

After determining your baseline and criteria for a major donor, separate major donors and prospects into meaningful and manageable segments, she says: "Zielinski Companies recommends creating tiers of major donors and prospects to care for each donor as personally as you can, while staying focused on those donors who will likely give the majority of funds in any given campaign or year."

Tier 1 donors are your top donors who rate high in capability and willingness in a consistent and strategic manner.

Tier 2 donors may be high in capacity or willingness, but likely not both.

Tier 3 prospects are those with whom you have some connection, who are known to have capacity, but haven't yet developed a deep knowledge of or interest in your organization.

Rank your major donors on their proximity to the gift, says Ehrlich, by asking:

- How close are they to giving?
- Have you been in touch with them recently?
- Have they been in touch with you recently?
- Have they hinted or stated that an outright gift might be coming?
- Do you know them well enough?
- Do you feel comfortable that you might receive a gift on the next call?

"Major donors are often rated initially on a two-part scale: willingness and capability," she says. "Willingness refers to a donor's connection to your organization and his or her level of interest and commitment to support the difference you are making in the community. Capability refers to a donor's financial capacity to support your organization."

Once you finish ranking your major donors, consider the capacity of your staff to manage those prospects, says Ehrlich: "A full-time major gifts officer can likely handle between 50 and 100 of your Tier 1 donors. Another 200 to 300 donors may fit into the Tier 2 segment. When functioning optimally, your nonprofit will be in touch in a meaningful way with all three tiers at least once a month. For Tier 1 donors and prospects, you'll need to create individualized strategies based on your knowledge of those individuals. For Tiers 2 and 3, you'll create group strategies that are as personalized as possible."

Source: Sandra G. Ehrlich, Director, Fund Development Services, Zielinski Companies, St. Louis, MO.
E-mail: sehrlich@zielinskico.com

Comprehensive Wealth Sweep Jump-starts Major Giving

When Patricia Laverty became manager of philanthropic giving at Rocky Mountain PBS (Denver, CO) in early 2010, she discovered the major gifts program barely scratched the surface in cultivating true major gifts. To kick-start the program, she used a comprehensive wealth sweep to mine major and planned-gift prospects from its 55,000-member database.

"We have a very large donor base because of our on-air fundraising and direct mail programs," says Laverty, "but finding major donors in this haystack is difficult."

She used the research firm Target Analytics®, a Blackbaud Company (Charleston, SC), to focus her efforts by analyzing her database. "Target Analytics uses publicly available financial data. The overlays that we purchased gave me likelihood ranges for both planned giving and major gifts," she says. "You can buy different products, and each one is a finer filter."

Rocky Mountain PBS used liquidity, hard assets, community connections and philanthropic donations screens to shake out 12,500 promising names from its database, with even more detailed liquidity information on 5,000 of those, and hard asset profiles on a further 500 names.

"Before we did the wealth screen," Laverty says, "I used our Cornerstone Society, which is a group of about 350 people who give to our local PBS network at a higher annual level, as my base to cultivate, but it was too small, and I found that some of these people were unable to become major donors."

The membership database used by many PBS stations includes interest codes for members that Laverty uses in developing personal relationships with prospects. "People want to give to something they're passionate about. When our producers come to me with a local program idea, I'm beginning to know who might be interested in sponsoring it."

Source: Patricia Laverty, Director of Philanthropic Giving, Rocky Mountain PBS, Denver, CO. E-mail: patricialaverty@rmpbs.org

How Ready Are You.... Really?

Use Predictive Modeling to Find Potential Donors

Prospect research and donor stewardship are about specific individuals — those who could donate or those who already have. Predictive modeling, in contrast, concerns generalized profiles, not individual people. By identifying attributes that correlate with an increased likelihood of giving, a predictive model creates a picture of a typical supporter, allowing an organization to make educated guesses about who will give and who will not.

Peter Wylie, a recognized expert in the field and author of "Data Mining for Fundraisers," answers questions about this area of fundraising that can be as misunderstood as it is promising:

In simple terms, what is predictive modeling in a fundraising context?

"Predictive modeling is basically a way of using data to build an algorithm, a score, that generates a profile of people who might not have given a lot of money yet, but look and act like the people who have. It's a way to know which lower-level givers your gift officers should be paying more attention to."

Can you give an example of what this would look like in practice?

"Say you're a university and you pull a Microsoft Excel file of 20,000 alumni records. You start by assigning attribute fields: 1) unique identification number, 2) total lifetime cash given, 3) a home phone appears in the database — yes or no, 4) business phone — yes or no, 5) e-mail — yes or no, 6) marital status, 7) preferred year of graduation, 8) ever attended any event after graduation — yes or no.

"Once you have that, you look for relationships between any field and the outcome variable, the amount of donation. Married donors will probably give more than single donors, for example, and widowed donors will give even more. So you assign a numerical score for each attribute, apply the formula to everybody in the database, and categorize people based on composite score. Some of the top scorers will already be under stewardship, but others you will never have heard of, and those are the people you want to introduce yourself to."

Is there a minimum number of donor records needed to generate meaningful results?

"Most small nonprofits either don't have something that could be considered a true donor database, and therefore, can't do predictive modeling, or they have thousands of files, which is plenty to make reliable decisions."

How do behavioral attributes like having attended a reunion compare in importance to demographic attributes like age or ZIP code?

"The more behaviors like opening an e-mail, attending an event or volunteering you can count, the better. Demographic information can be behavioral, but it doesn't have to be. Someone might have given you their business phone, but a gift officer might have just looked it up. Someone might have given you their mailing address, but you might have acquired it somewhere."

Are there data points nonprofits should be tracking but often aren't?

"Electronic data is one of the biggest areas. At any event where people are using membership cards — a museum, a symphony, a ticketed fundraiser — there is data that can be stored — so much that you can learn quite quickly what kinds of events people go to, what subject areas they prefer and so on. All this can then be correlated to donations.

"The other big area is web metrics — tracking the relationship between online behaviors — opening certain kinds of e-mails, visiting certain parts of a website — and giving habits. This is a promising field, but its challenge is that website software often gives aggregated data instead of personalized."

What steps might an organization take in exploring predictive modeling?

"A good first step is just seeing if you can pull information out of your database and put it into spreadsheet format. You can do some pretty good initial analysis without even needing a statistical software package. Reading the CoolData blog would also be helpful."

Source: Peter Wylie, Author, Data Mining for Fundraisers, Washington, D.C. E-mail: pbradwylie@aol.com

Methods for Assessing a Donor's Giving Potential

The ability to determine a person's net worth for the purposes of fundraising is a myth that has been perpetuated for years. Even if you know the majority of a person's assets, you most likely will not know all of his or her liabilities. And you have to know both to know the net worth.

That doesn't mean you can't estimate an individual's raw capability to donate. There are a number of formulas and guides available for this purpose, and trial and error may be needed to figure out the best one for your constituents.

Following is a sampling of some of the more popular assessment methods, including some hypothetical examples, illustrated at right. Just remember, you still have to convince the person to give to your cause.

In seeking to assess a donor's giving potential, keep in mind:

1. Liquidity is key, unless you are looking for donations of property. Even stock holdings may not be available for donations in certain circumstances.

2. Annual gifts are generally based on income and capital gifts are based on assets.

3. Consider age, number and ages of children, lifestyle, and cost of living for the location.

4. Only stock holdings for insiders and owners of 5 percent and above are reported and available as public information.

5. Assets held in trusts are difficult to find through research.

6. Information on executives and directors of public companies is much more readily available. Proxy statements can be very helpful in identifying income, stock holdings, company loans, retirement plans and other indications of wealth.

7. Those in real estate and agriculture are often land-rich and cash-poor.

8. Owners of private companies may be putting all of their earnings back into the company. On the other hand, they may be getting additional perks from this affiliation, such as home allowances, cars, paid vacations, etc., that would offset usual living expenses and leave them with more liquidity.

9. The ownership of valuable property can be expensive to maintain. This includes lavish homes, ranches, art collections, cars, boats, etc. Consider property taxes, insurance, hired staff, and other costs as liabilities when figuring assets and worth. Remember that assessed value may have no relationship to purchase price or market value.

10. Stock brokers and investors usually have a higher proportion of their wealth in stocks and bonds. Venture capitalists generally have more cash, but it may be tied up in investments.

11. Income estimates are available for many professions in several sources.

12. Ratings and net worth estimates are available from several electronic screening vendors. Ask how they arrive at their figures before using the data.

Content not available in this edition

Four Rules of Thumb for Estimating Major Prospects' Assets

Prospect research seeks many kinds of information, but few carry as much weight as a prospect's total net worth. All other information is judged in relation to this gold standard.

Unfortunately, net worth is information that no prospect research system will fully uncover, says David Lamb, senior consultant at Target Analytics, a Blackbaud company (Charleston, SC).

However, he says it is something that can be estimated, and he offers the following estimation methods:

- 5 to 10 percent of annual income
- (Total real estate) x (4) x (5 percent, when real estate value is greater than $500,000)
- (Total stock holdings) x (4) x (5 percent, when stock value is greater than $100,000)
- 5 percent of all known assets, when assets are greater than $1 million

These simple rules of thumb are based on national averages and will produce only rough estimates of net worth. Nevertheless, Lamb says the figures they generate provide a suitable starting point for conversations with major donors. "You know you'll at least be in the right ballpark, and you can go from there," he says.

Source: David Lamb, Senior Consultant, Target Analytics, Parker, CO. E-mail: david.lamb@blackbaud.com

Go Into Prospect Research With Realistic Expectations

Prospect research can reveal a great deal of information, but like anything else, it has its limitations. Having realistic expectations will help you avoid frustration and make the research process more efficient and productive.

David Lamb, senior consultant at Target Analytics, offers the following thoughts on what prospect research can and can't do.

What you might be able to find:
- Where does your prospect live?
- Does she/he own property?
- Where does your prospect work?
- Does that employment contribute to gift capacity?
- Does the prospect give elsewhere? How much?
- Where is your prospect connected in the community?

What you will never know:
- Your prospect's net worth
- The size of his/her bank account
- Most investments
- Inheritances or family money
- Almost anything the prospect wants to keep private

Form Measures Prospect's Ability, Likelihood to Give

Here's another example of a prospect rating form. This form serves as a way to measure both an individual's ability to and likelihood of making a major gift.

Criteria used to rate prospects on this form include:

1. **Common interests.** Does the prospect exhibit interest in the objectives your organization attempts to address?
2. **Financial ability.** Can the prospect afford to make what you consider to be a major gift?
3. **Commitment to philanthropy.** Does the prospect have a giving history?
4. **Commitment to your organization.** Has the prospect exhibited any past commitment to your organization?
5. **Linkages with your organization.** Has the prospect held an office with your nonprofit or been served as a client of your organization? Does he/she have friends or family who have linkage to you?
6. **Time window.** Is the time right for the prospect to make a major gift?
7. **Personality.** How can the individual's personality effect his/her interest in making a gift? Is the individual driven by a strong ego? Is he/she caring? Personality traits will influence the likelihood of giving.
8. **Past solicitation success.** Has the prospect contributed in the past? Is there a long or brief history of giving? Has she/he made a previous major gift?

9. **Common politics/philosophy.** Do the political/philosophical beliefs of this individual coincide with the organization's mission and goals? Does the prospect stand far to the left or right politically?

Weights are assigned to each rating criteria and then added. In this case, the highest possible score one can receive is 85.

Content not available in this edition

Ask the Right Questions in Major Gift Discovery Calls

Discovery calls are key to keeping a donor pipeline stocked and healthy, says Eli Jordfald, senior major gifts director at UNC Lineberger Comprehensive Cancer Center (Chapel Hill, NC).

"A discovery call is a call to a prospective donor — someone who may or may not have given in the past — with the aim of finding out if cultivation toward a major gift is appropriate," Jordfald says. "The goal of the call is not necessarily to get a visit, but to determine if a visit is warranted.

"Past donors who have consistently given at lower levels are a great constituency for discovery calls," she says. "Other groups include first-time donors who have given several hundred dollars, individuals who have given generously to causes similar to yours, and individuals who have been suggested by board members or other major donors."

Jordfald advises fundraisers to approach discovery calls as an opportunity to listen, not talk. She also suggests structuring the conversation around three sets of questions:

1. **Questions that assess interest in the organization, including:**
   - "Tell me about your experiences with our organization."
   - "Would you be interested in learning more about our research and programs?"
   - "How do you see your involvement with the work of our organization?"

2. **Questions assessing financial capacity, including:**
   - "Where do you work and in what capacity?"
   - "Do you have plans to travel?"
   - "Do you have favorite organizations you like to support? Tell me about your involvement there."

3. **Questions that determine next steps, including:**
   - "Would it be convenient for me to visit you in a week or two?"
   - "I'd like to invite you on a tour of our facilities. Would you like to schedule a time to do that?"

For organizations embarking on a discovery call program, Jordfald recommends incorporating calls into a weekly schedule. Above all, she says, just enjoy the conversations. "It's really a lot of fun to talk with people who are interested in your organization. When you ask the right questions, you'll be amazed how many wonderful and informative conversations you will have. It's a great use of time."

Source: Eli Jordfald, Senior Major Gifts Director, UNC Lineberger Comprehensive Cancer Center, Chapel Hill, NC. E-mail: eli_jordfald@med.unc.edu

Debunking Discovery Call Myths

Discovery calls are plagued by misunderstandings, says Eli Jordfald, senior major gifts director at UNC Lineberger Comprehensive Cancer Center (Chapel Hill, NC). Here she takes on some of the most common discovery call myths.

✓ **Myth:** The purpose of a discovery call is to get an appointment.
Reality: The purpose of the call is to determine if a visit is warranted. "Realizing that an appointment is not the sole goal of the call is a real aha moment for many people," says Jordfald. "It shifts the whole focus of the call and takes a lot of the pressure off."

✓ **Myth:** You should not immediately disclose the reason for the call.
Reality: Clearly stating one's title and organizational role prevents misunderstandings and makes the conversation much more productive, says Jordfald.

✓ **Myth:** You should never ask for a gift in a discovery call.
Reality: In cases where a person is interested but not a major gift prospect, offering lower-level fundraising priorities is perfectly acceptable. "Your primary objective is finding out if a personal visit is appropriate, but often it is not, and there is no reason not to seek smaller gifts," says Jordfald.

✓ **Myth:** You should not use a calling script.
Reality: "You want to be warm and conversational, but you need to be sure you ask certain questions or make certain points, and a script or outline is the best way to do that," says Jordfald.

Case Statement Prep

- In drafting your case statement, delineate ways in which the realization of your strategic plan will not only assist those you serve, but positively impact your community.
- Focus your case statement's message on your organization's future rather than on campaign goals.

Case Statement Essentials

- When preparing your organization's case statement, keep the four C's in mind: a case statement should be clear, concise, convincing and compelling.

PRE-CAMPAIGN

How Ready Are You.... Really?

Develop a Persuasive Case Statement

A nonprofit's strategic plan serves as the "parent" to the case statement. The case statement documents the organization's vision and makes a compelling case for its funding. All subsequent campaign materials are an outgrowth of the case statement.

Because its purpose is often misunderstood, we've identified some principles that will guide you as you develop your next case statement:

- ☐ The process of writing a case statement, and involving prospects in drafting it, is at least as important as the finished product.
- ☐ The document should effectively communicate leadership's vision for the organization.
- ☐ It should reflect the institution's mission and be an outgrowth of the organization's strategic plan.
- ☐ A case statement forces agreement regarding an organization's priorities.
- ☐ It identifies genuine needs and offers practical solutions for meeting those needs.

- ☐ It should convey urgency.
- ☐ The completed case statement ensures that all constituents receive consistent messages about the organization's vision and priorities.
- ☐ The document identifies key themes and messages that will be useful in developing additional campaign materials, proposals and presentations.
- ☐ The case statement should be market driven — it should talk about satisfying donors' needs instead of the institution's needs.
- ☐ It should present a positive image of your organization.
- ☐ It should build on the organization's potential rather than past accomplishments.
- ☐ It should involve prospects.
- ☐ The document should demonstrate how gifts being sought will unleash the organization's potential and turn dreams into reality.
- ☐ It should be readable and credible.
- ☐ The case statement should provide a clear link between an organization's mission, its vision and funding opportunities.

How to Sell Your Vision to Donor Prospects

Behavioral research shows that donors are fundamentally skeptical about donating to nonprofits, says Tom Ahern, author and principle of Ahern Communications, Ink (Foster, RI). "The most ancient parts of our brain are concerned only with survival," Ahern says, "and they need a very compelling reason to part with hard-earned money."

A concise and compelling case statement is key to providing this reason, he says. Here, Ahern discusses some of the fine points of this important solicitation tool:

What is the bedrock of a successful case statement?

"Everything in a good case statement is focused on answering three key questions: Why this organization? Why now? Why should I care? You need to explain why your project is uniquely valuable and more worthy of investment than other projects. You need to explain why the donor should write a check today instead of next week or next year. And you need to explain why the donor should care about what your vision is and what you are trying to do."

How should a case statement be used? What is it designed to do?

"A case statement is a tool to be used in face-to-face solicitation. You don't send it to the prospect in advance; you bring it with you to the meeting. You have it in your hands to prompt the points you want to focus on, and you might open it up at times to illustrate a point or have the prospect look at something. When the meeting is over, the case statement can also be left with the prospect as he or she is considering a gift."

What does a good case statement look like? Pages of text? A short list of bulleted points?

"There is no formulaic answer, but in general you want to make the statement as short as possible. The core case for Yale's $3.2 billion Yale>>Tomorrow campaign was only 550 words. The rest of the document was pages and pages of photographs and provocative quotes about how uncertain the world can be and how important it is to plan for the future."

Development professionals have a great deal of information about their organization. What kinds of facts should be included in a case statement?

"There are two basic types of evidence: statistical and anecdotal. Research shows that donors respond far more strongly to one anecdote about one person than to any amount of statistics. Stats should be used, but as a background that reinforces the central narrative. It's also important to know that research has shown people respond much more strongly to the story of a single child than the story of that child and a sibling. Adding even one other person to an anecdote makes it less effective, and adding more than that just crushes donor response."

What's the biggest misconception nonprofits have about making their case with prospects?

"Talking too much about themselves. People don't give to charities, they give through them. Unfortunately, charities often forget they are only a means for a donor to help solve a problem. I have seen case statements asking for $150 million in which the donor is never mentioned, the word 'you' is never used. That is not an engaging practice and not a good way to get support."

Source: Tom Ahern, Principle, Ahern Communications, Ink, Foster, RI. E-mail: A2Bmail@aol.com

Involve Constituents in Crafting Your Case Statement

Crafting a case statement for your major fundraising campaign? Involve key volunteers and donors, along with a slice of your community, as much as possible, says Vice President for Advancement Wayne Webster, Ripon College (Ripon, WI).

Ripon is in the silent phase of an upcoming comprehensive campaign, with officials having already secured more than $9.5 million in gifts, largely with the help of board members and other key constituents.

Webster shares steps Ripon officials took to involve key players every step of the way, along with how those steps benefited the campaign as a whole:

1. **Refine your case statement.** Board members and Ripon's president held briefings with select individuals, tweaking the case statement in response to their feedback.

2. **Complete a feasibility study.** Feedback from Ripon's study, completed by a consulting firm, revealed which aspects of the case statement resonated with people and gave them a general idea of how much money they could raise for each area of need.

3. **Involve board members early on.** Senior administration worked with the board of trustees' advancement committee to tweak language and help create the vision for the case statement. Webster says this led to many of them making early leadership commitments because they believe in the case and helped to shape it.

4. **Secure early gifts and buy time.** Ripon created a 12-member steering committee of board members who will make commitments first, then help solicit other top prospects in the silent phase. This gives major and planned gift staff another year to focus on the next tier of donors to put the campaign over the top once it goes public.

5. **Provide information and answers.** Webster says members of the director's group within the Advancement Division play a critical role in providing answers to the committee, whose members will also participate in a daylong campaign training session.

Source: Wayne P. Webster, Vice President for Advancement, Ripon College, Ripon, WI. E-mail: WebsterW@ripon.edu

Six Ways to Make Your Case Statement More Compelling

The case statement serves as an important tool in preparing for a capital campaign. This printed document should provide compelling justification to support your effort as both key donors and prospects share in its development or in reviewing it prior to the launch of a capital campaign.

To make your case statement as persuading as possible, incorporate these principles into its development:

1. **Illustrate your organization's strength and ability to forge ahead with confidence.** Donors and prospects first need to be assured of your institution's viability. Do you have a solid history of balanced budgets? Is your endowment growing? Have you followed through on past plans? It's important your organization's history demonstrates you are worthy of future support.

2. **Create a strategic plan that knocks their socks off.** To generate extraordinary gifts you need to get people's attention with extraordinary but attainable plans. Create a long-term strategic plan for your organization that exemplifies your intent to make significant achievements and be a leader.

3. **Tie your organization's future to quantifiable objectives.** Don't simply say: "We want to build a great university," but rather, include clear objectives that show how you intend to build a great university. What are the quantifiable outcomes of becoming "great," and how will you get there?

4. **Spell out how your long-term plans relate to your mission and what a difference their fulfillment will make in the lives of those you serve.** It's important to stay true to your organization's purpose. If not, perhaps you should re-examine your mission statement before developing new plans and preparing for a campaign.

5. **Paint a clear picture of how gift revenue will be used.** Be up front with potential investors. Show them exactly how gifts will be used and include the cost of each project. Prospects are more likely to invest if they fully understand your plans.

6. **Don't be hesitant to share the consequences of not fulfilling your plans.** While the overall theme of your case statement should be positive, it's acceptable to convey what will happen (or not happen) if your plans are not fully realized. This distinction brings urgency to the need for a campaign.

The case statement in and of itself will not invoke major gifts. It will, however, capture the attention of would-be donors and play a key role in the solicitation process.

Why Conduct a Feasibility Study?

The feasibility or planning study is an important part of any pre-campaign effort.

A feasibility study involves a series of confidential one-on-one interviews, often conducted by a third-party fundraising consultant and directed at major gift prospects to better understand their perceptions of your organization and the degree to which they might become involved, both financially and as volunteers.

The process of engaging board members, as well as past

Feasibility Study Is a Pre-campaign Must!

Once you've completed the first phase of determining whether you're justified in pursuing a capital campaign, based on: 1) genuine and fundable needs, 2) an adequate and capable donor constituency, 3) adequate resources to implement and carry out a campaign, 4) a convinced and committed board, and 5) a competent and prepared staff, it's time to pursue the second pre-campaign phase — the feasibility study.

Although the method of conducting feasibility studies may vary among nonprofits, as well as among consultants, their aims are quite similar. For the most part, feasibility studies involve a series of questions directed to both past donors and potential contributors in an effort to better understand their perceptions of an organization and determine their likelihood to participate and possible degree of involvement in a capital campaign. The completion of a feasibility study will help answer the following questions:

❑ **Does the cause have validity and appeal?**
Answers to these questions will demonstrate the donor's perceptions of your organization and should provide some insight into the personal interests of the donor that will be helpful in tailoring a proposal for a specific portion of your campaign.

❑ **How much can you expect to raise?**
Although the feasibility study is not intended to serve as a solicitation for campaign pledges, questions can be worded to determine the prospect's willingness to participate as well as what anticipated range of giving the prospect may consider contributing over a specified period of time. Although there is no specified number of prospects to be interviewed during the feasibility study, it makes sense to involve as many of your top prospects as possible; as much as 80 percent of your campaign goal will come from as few as 20 percent of your donor constituency. In fact, many of today's major campaigns result in even greater amounts coming from an even smaller percentage of the constituency.

and would-be donors in these interview sessions, serves to:
- Cultivate key prospects in preparation for the ask.
- Help persons feel valuable to the organization.
- Allow the anonymous expression of dissatisfaction.
- Test the marketplace for dollar support and leadership.
- Provide the opportunity to proceed with a campaign for a reduced goal if the desired goal isn't possible.
- Provide a way to assess the charity's health in areas which affect its ability to raise campaign support.

❑ **How long will it take, and how much will it cost?**
Answers to feasibility questions will not only help determine how much can be raised, but also how long it might take. This is where the expertise of a consultant can be particularly helpful in recommending: 1) a campaign goal, 2) whether the capital campaign should be incorporated with or separate from the annual campaign, 3) what kinds of gifts should count toward the goal (e.g., planned gifts, real or personal property, cash only, etc.), 4) the scale of gifts required to achieve the goal, and 5) the readiness of the organization to launch a campaign.

❑ **Do you have the board and volunteer leadership to get the job done?**
Both board members and key volunteers should be a part of the feasibility questioning. If board members' pledges are to be a key part of the campaign goal, their commitment should be obvious. Likewise, successful completion of the campaign will take a great deal of volunteer time. The feasibility study will help identify levels of volunteer commitment.

Completion of the feasibility study will strengthen the case for support using comments received throughout the study. It will also begin cultivating the interest of your top donors, and you will better understand the competition for funds in your community (or region) and how your case stacks up. Finally, the study demonstrates that you are serious about efforts to improve funding and also shows what top prospects think of you.

The successful completion of a feasibility study will result in a recommendation to the full board regarding a realistic yet challenging goal, the intended use of funds to be raised, and the campaign's format.

How Ready Are You.... Really?

How to Begin a Planning Study for a Major Capital Campaign

When considering a major capital campaign, many nonprofits turn to outside counsel to perform a campaign feasibility or planning study. A consultant interviews the people/businesses most likely to support a capital campaign and makes a recommendation about how much they believe your organization could potentially raise.

How do you choose the best consultant for this important task?

The first step is knowing when your organization is ready to take that first step and hire a consultant, says John M. Bouza, president and founder of the fundraising consultant firm, CanFund, The Canadian Centre for Fundraising (Ottawa, Ontario, Canada).

"Consultants are experts in their fields ... blessed with imagination," says Bouza. "As outsiders to your organization, consultants can judge its strengths and weaknesses with objectivity, see beyond the day-to-day routine and can help you position your organization for long-term growth."

Bouza says nonprofits may consider hiring a consultant under these circumstances:

✓ When you are embarking on a new method of fundraising, such as direct mail, a capital campaign or a planned giving program — especially if your organization has outgrown past, fundraising activities and needs to transform itself into a larger, stable and professionally managed organization.

✓ When outside circumstances or opportunities suddenly call for more efficient and effectual fundraising, such as the planning of a new facility, the sudden need for increased visibility, or the potential for a campaign-starting endowment.

✓ When hiring or reinvigorating fundraising staff, you may need a consultant to supervise the selection process or to oversee training sessions.

Once your organization has decided to hire a consultant, Bouza says to create a request for proposal (RFP) to let prospects understand your organization and its needs fully before engaging in business together. For details on doing so, see the box, below.

Source: John M. Bouza, President and Founder, CanFund, The Canadian Centre for Fundraising, Ottawa, Ontario, Canada. E-mail: jbouza@canfund.org

---

Request For Proposal Leads to Best Consultant Match

Looking to hire a consultant to perform a feasibility or planning study for an upcoming capital fundraising campaign? John M. Bouza, president and founder of CanFund, The Canadian Centre for Fundraising (Ottawa, Ontario, Canada) says a Request for Proposal (RFP) will help you identify the consulting firm or organization that will best work with you. An effective RFP, Bouza says, should:

❑ Describe your charity or nonprofit.

❑ Describe the project/purpose for which funds are needed.

❑ Identify that you are requesting RFPs from qualified firms or organizations to conduct a planning or feasibility study in preparation for the proposed capital campaign.

❑ Ask submitting firms/organizations to:

✓ Identify their interest in conducting the feasibility study (and the subsequent capital campaign).

✓ Describe their experience in similar studies/campaigns.

✓ Identify their expert personnel and who would actually do the study.

✓ Describe their proposed methodology for conducting the study.

✓ Describe, in general terms, their usual methodology for conducting the subsequent campaign in the event that the study recommends a campaign proceed.

✓ Note the time frame and ability to meet it.

✓ List several references with phone numbers.

✓ Document proposed fees. On what basis are they calculated? What is included in professional fees? What additional costs will there be? (Generally quoted as an all inclusive project rather than an hourly rate.)

❑ State how, on what basis, and by whom the decision will be made to retain a particular firm or organization.

❑ Will a short-list of candidates be invited for interviews? When and with whom will they meet? (This is vital to a good selection process).

❑ Clearly state the planned time frame for receipt of submissions, decision about whom to hire, when study needs to take place, and when study needs to be completed (generally two to three months).

❑ State that the decision to retain any or none of the submitted applications is the sole prerogative of your institution; that the decision will be based on a number of factors and cost will not be the sole factor (e.g., the contract need not necessarily go to the lowest bidder).

PRE-CAMPAIGN

How Ready Are You.... Really?

Feasibility Study Should Include a Definitive Timeline

When you're about to conduct a feasibility or planning study in anticipation of a capital campaign, it's critical that you use a timeline that delineates who does what and when.

Often staff have not been involved with a feasibility study, so a timeline helps all stakeholders visualize exactly what needs to take place and makes all parties involved accountable for their respective parts in the process.

While many variations of feasibility timelines exist, this sample can help you develop an appropriate timeline of your own. Remember to include the duration of each phase along with specific dates, tasks and names of persons responsible for each task:

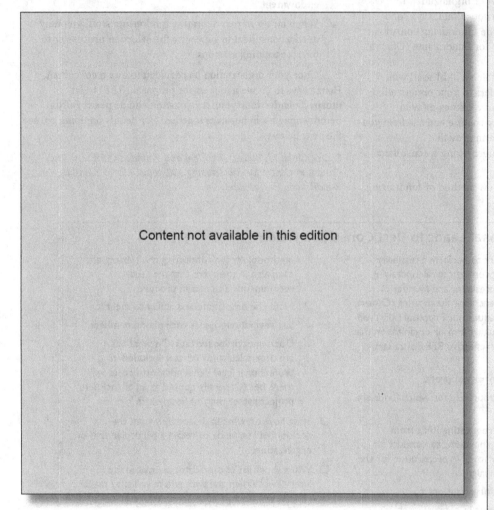

Content not available in this edition

Justify the Decision to Not Conduct Study

Feasibility studies are a crucial component of numerous large-dollar capital campaigns. They shape the campaign's framework, identify its major stakeholders and refine its case statement.

Yet many nonprofits (mostly smaller ones) conduct perfectly successful campaigns with no formal planning study. And many other organizations find themselves somewhere in the middle — considering a study, but not convinced it is necessary for them.

If your organization falls in this latter category, consider crafting a rationale for not conducting a study. If you are leaning away from a feasibility study, articulate the reasons why this makes strategic sense for your organization. Will your campaign be so small a study would offer limited benefit? Will your campaign be relying on a small number of funding sources or targeting just a few granting institutions? Do you simply not have the budget to commission a study?

Taking the time to answer these questions in writing will bring many important issues into focus. Maybe you will decide that a feasibility study would be appropriate and beneficial after all. Maybe you will be confirmed in your sense that a study is not right for your organization at this time. Whatever the final decision, you can be assured that the critical thought demanded by the decision-making process will benefit your campaign in the long run.

Successful Capital Campaigns: From Start to Finish, Third Edition.
Edited by Scott C. Stevenson.
© 2012 Stevenson, Inc. Published 2012 by Stevenson, Inc.

Successful Capital Campaigns: From Start to Finish — 3rd Edition

Setting the Size, Scope and Campaign Duration

Once all the research has been completed or is nearing completion — you have identified and researched prospects, you have identified and prioritized funding opportunities, you have completed an internal audit to determine your readiness and you have completed a thorough planning study — you can begin to put paint brush to canvas and prepare a campaign plan that is uniquely yours, complete with goals, gift ranges, funding priorities, start and end dates, volunteer structure and more.

Understand the Science of Determining Funding Priorities

Setting fundraising priorities is a crucial prerequisite to raising major gifts.

Here, Brian Sheridan, development and marketing manager at the Los Angeles and San Gabriel Rivers Watershed Council (Los Angeles, CA), which works to preserve and enhance the watershed's economic and ecological vitality, discusses factors all nonprofits must keep in mind when determining funding priorities:

Is there a one-size-fits-all model for determining funding priorities?

"No. However, there is a one-size-fits-99-percent-of-all-nonprofits model. Board involvement in fundraising and individual donations is key. Individual giving should be emphasized and re-emphasized. Every board member should be responsible for bringing in resources."

What are some of the key components in any model for determining a nonprofit's fundraising priorities?

"Your model should differentiate between restricted grants and unrestricted sources of funds. In this day of diminishing endowments and tax base, we also have to plan for the eventuality that either of these sources will go down. If we have not diversified, it leaves us with two choices: cut programs or operate in the red. If we have to cut successful programs, then we aren't doing our duty as nonprofits. If we operate in the red, we will only last for so long. Individual donors can provide a critical base of funding and don't require the level of benefits a sponsor does."

What components should be figured into a nonprofits' model that often are not?

"I think a lot of organizations overlook the value of being included in wills and bequests. I think this is because it is a longer-term payoff, but the benefits can be substantial."

How should a nonprofit determine what kinds of manpower (executive director, board of directors, development director, etc.) will take ownership of its funding priorities?

"Be wary of the development committee or anything else that takes fundraising ownership away from the board. The last thing you want is for the board to say, 'I don't need to fundraise — that's what the development/gala/fundraising/etc. committee is doing.'"

What advice would you give to a nonprofit that is trying to determine what is most needed versus what is most fundable?

"Be careful of chasing the money. When you chase the available funds, you often get a partially funded project, which is expensive to an organization and difficult to pull off. Before you begin budgeting for a program, make sure to have an anchor funder who you are fairly certain will fund the project before going after smaller requests."

Source: Brian Sheridan, Development and Marketing Manager, Los Angeles and San Gabriel Rivers Watershed Council, Los Angeles, CA. E-mail: brian@lasgrwc.org

Look to Current Donors When Setting a Campaign Goal

You can use various guidelines and procedures to determine an appropriate capital campaign goal. And no one guideline should be used exclusively as a determining factor.

That being said, here's one guideline that will provide insight into an appropriate campaign goal for your organization:

1. Take the campaign goal under consideration and divide that by the total number of contributors for the most recent year.

2. Compare that number to the previous year's average-sized gift to your annual fund (total amount raised last year divided by number of donors).

If the per-person contribution for your proposed campaign is 10 times greater than your actual average gift size from your most recent fiscal year, your campaign goal is probably on target.

EXAMPLE		
Capital Campaign Goal Under Consideration		$5 million
Total donors last year		2,000
Average gift size	$	2,500
Amount of Annual Fund Gifts Raised Last Year	$	500,000
Total donors last year		2,000
Average gift size	$	250
Capital Campaign Average Gift Size	$	2,500
Annual Fund Average Gift Size	$	250

Setting the Size, Scope and Campaign Duration

Prioritize Funding Projects Before Launching a Campaign

Your organization may need its electrical system rewired, but it would no doubt be unwise to fund the project with a campaign. Why? Because it has little or no appeal to prospective donors.

On the other hand, you may be able to raise significant gifts for a new swimming pool complex because of its popularity, but is that your nonprofit's most pressing need?

A Project Analysis Rating Scale provides one way of measuring and prioritizing which potential campaign projects are most needed and most apt to receive funding from your constituency.

Here's how it works: First, identify those needs perceived to be most critical by your employees and assign a cost to each project. It would be wise to include some board members and major gift prospects in the process of identifying greatest needs. That way, they will begin to own and perhaps, fund one or more of those needs at the appropriate time.

After identifying critical needs (as perceived internally), rank each project separately on the Project Analysis Rating Scale. Criteria used to rate and prioritize each project includes:

- **Internal importance** — Among all of your organization's needs, how does this project rank?

- **Donor "attractiveness"** — How attractive would this project be to potential donors? Is it, for instance, the type of project that would evoke strong emotion (like replacing a torn-down church steeple)?

- **Number of prospects** — Would the project have appeal to a large or small number of prospects?

- **Prospects' financial ability** — Can you judge the financial ability of your prospect pool based on this project compared to the ability of a different group of prospects interested in another project? For instance, let's assume you represent a college and you're measuring the fundability of a new social work lab as opposed to a new biology lab. The proposed biology lab prospect pool (which would include alumni who are medical professionals), would probably have greater financial ability than the social work alumni constituency.

- **Impact of completed project** — How many lives will the completed project affect?

- **Visibility of completed project** — Will the completion of the project be noticed by those you serve? Will it help your nonprofit to better market its services?

Each criterion should be assigned a number based on your perception. That number is then multiplied by a weight factor. The results are then added to give an overall ranking of the project's fundability and need as compared to other possible campaign projects.

The highest score a project could receive, based on this model, is 60 and the lowest possible score would be 12. The projects with a 60 rating would be the most likely candidates for a campaign.

Content not available in this edition

Setting the Size, Scope and Campaign Duration

Anticipate Sources of Campaign Gifts Up Front

Several factors go into planning a successful capital campaign — writing the case statement, completing the feasibility or planning study, creating a scale of gifts, rating and screening prospects and more. The odds of your campaign being a success will increase with a higher level of upfront planning.

One variable that should be a part of pre-campaign planning — but sometimes gets overlooked — is anticipating the source of your gifts. Projecting the percentage

of gifts that will come from each constituency source will help focus priorities in terms of required staff expertise, best use of available time and specific fundraising strategies.

Be able to project the percentage of campaign support from each of your constituencies early in your campaign planning. Here is one charity's source projections:

Board Members (Current and Past) — 15 to 30 percent
Individuals — 60 to 65 percent
Businesses — 20 percent
Foundations/Corporations — 5 to 10 percent

Begin by Plugging in Prospect Names

How do you determine a challenging yet realistic campaign goal for your organization?

As you draw closer to launching a campaign, a feasibility study will give some indication of giving levels at which prospects see themselves. Long before that feasibility (or planning) study, you should have an idea of your fundraising effort's scope.

Begin by creating a scale of gifts planning chart. (See Scale of Gifts Planning Chart, below) Knowing that as much as 80 to 95 percent of your goal will come from as few as 5 percent of your constituency, you can begin to identify which prospects might fit into each gift range. This chart is based on a 6:1 prospect-to-donor ratio.

Once you have devised such a chart, you can begin to review your list of prospect names, plugging them into those levels you believe they are likely to give, based on both financial capability and likelihood of giving at those levels. (See Top Prospects Review form, right.) Although your initial planning may not include plugging names into the lowest ranges, identifying prospects in the top ranges will help to reveal whether the goal you have chosen is on (or off) the mark.

TOP PROSPECTS REVIEW
As of _____ (date)

$1,000,000 Range
Needed Prospects: 6

1. _____
2. _____
3. _____
4. _____
5. _____
6. _____

$500,000-999,999
Needed Prospects: 12

1. _____
2. _____
3. _____
4. _____
5. _____
6. _____
7. _____
8. _____
9. _____
10. _____
11. _____
12. _____

And so on.....

SCALE OF GIFTS PLANNING CHART

Scale of Gifts Needed to Secure $5 Million
Based on 100 Gifts of $10,000 and Above

Gift Range	Prospects Needed	Gifts Needed	Amount
$ 1,000,000	6	1	$1,000,000
$ 500,000-999,999	12	2	$1,000,000
$ 250,000-499,000	24	4	$1,000,000
$ 100,000-249,999	30	5	$500,000
$ 50,000-99,999	60	10	$500,000
$ 25,000-49,999	120	20	$500,000
$ 10,000-24,999	300	50	$500,000
	552	92	$5,000,000

Setting the Size, Scope and Campaign Duration

Scale-of-gifts Model Crucial for Success

A scale-of-gifts model serves a crucial role in maintaining focus throughout the duration of a capital campaign. Whether you're attempting to raise $500,000 or $50 million, the scale-of-gifts model helps illustrate both the number and size of gifts needed to achieve campaign success.

Such a model also helps to monitor progress throughout a campaign's solicitation phase.

While a thorough feasibility or planning study will provide the basis for your own scale-of-gifts model, answering four key questions will help you customize a model that addresses your organization's unique circumstances:

1. What do you consider to be a challenging yet attainable goal?

2. To whom will your campaign be directed? Are you seeking out anyone willing to contribute at any level, or do you only want gifts of a certain size?

3. What is the size of your existing prospect pool?

4. How much have you raised in previous campaigns? What were the largest gifts, and how many participated at each level of gifts?

Once you address these questions, you are ready to design your own scale-of-gifts model. In doing so, however, keep these two key principles in mind: a) as much as 90 percent of your goal will come from 10 percent of your prospect pool, and b) on average, you will need six prospects for each successful call (within each gift range).

Design two or three model alternatives such as those shown here and discuss them with persons most intimately involved with your campaign (e.g., staff, board members, top volunteers). Once you have agreed upon a model, stick to it. Keep the model constantly before everyone involved with soliciting gifts. It will serve as your guide throughout the campaign.

Create a Workable Campaign Pyramid in Seconds

Careful planning and realistic goal setting are crucial to any successful capital campaign. Campaign pyramids calculating the number and size of gifts needed to achieve campaign objectives are invaluable in this regard, but the number-crunching required to build them can daunt even the most numerically minded officials.

Fortunately help has arrived. Blackbaud's Gift Range Calculator uses widely accepted industry standards to calculate a workable campaign pyramid in seconds. Just enter your total campaign goal and hit the "calculate" button to get a detailed breakdown of the gifts and prospects required at various levels, along with cumulative totals and percentages.

Though off-the-shelf results like these should serve as the starting point for more detailed conversations, the Gift Range Calculator can be a great help in the initial stages of campaign planning.

Sample results from a hypothetical $2 million campaign.

Gift Range	No. Gifts required	No. Prospects required	Subtotal	Cumulative total	Cumulative percentage
		Goal Amount: 2000000			
200,000.00	1	4	200,000.00	200,000.00	10%
150,000.00	1	4	150,000.00	350,000.00	18%
100,000.00	2	8	200,000.00	550,000.00	28%
75,000.00	3	12	225,000.00	775,000.00	39%
50,000.00	5	20	250,000.00	1,025,000.00	51%
38,000.00	8	32	304,000.00	1,329,000.00	66%
25,000.00	10	40	250,000.00	1,579,000.00	79%
13,000.00	12	48	156,000.00	1,735,000.00	87%
5,000.00	12	48	60,000.00	1,795,000.00	90%
Under 5,000.00	82	328	205,000.00	2,000,000.00	100%
Totals	136	544		2,000,000.00	

PRE-CAMPAIGN   Setting the Size, Scope and Campaign Duration

Can Your Board Fund a Third of Your Campaign Goal?

Case Study: *You want to launch a major campaign in 2015, but there's a problem. You have a board made up mostly of individuals who have neither the capacity nor the inclination to make major gifts. What to do?*

First of all, you need to know that it's not uncommon for a successful campaign to realize anywhere from one-third to one-half of its goal from both current and former board members. So you have three years to transform your board into a precedent-setting group of generous donors. Can it be done? With focus and determination, yes.

Here's a very basic outline of what you'll need to do:

1. First, identify any current and former board members who have the capability to make a significant gift. If you come up with no one, evaluate your charity's pool of nonboard donors to identify such a person or persons.

2. Begin to cultivate that individual or handful of individuals about the need for methodically and selectively recruiting financially capable board members. If they are not already on your board, do what's necessary to get them elected.

3. Help those few insiders realize their primary goal is to identify, cultivate and recruit others of means who will join your board and become actively engaged in its work.

4. At the same time this handful of members is working to stack the deck, ask them to begin pressuring existing board members by proposing minimum annual contributions. This forces current board members to either rise to the occasion or resign.

Although the process of transforming a board is much more complex than the steps outlined here, seeing it described in this simplistic manner can help you to begin to tackle the board transformation challenge head on.

Incorporate Planned Giving Into Capital Campaigns

Planned gifts can be a source of great revenue and are being pursued in a wider variety of contexts. While nonprofits often talk about incorporating planned giving into their campaign goals, very few actually do so with any degree of success, says Kevin Johnson, principal of Retriever Development Counsel (Portland, OR).

Part of the challenge is the difference of purpose between legacy and capital gifts, says Johnson. "The biggest value of a capital campaign is its single-minded focus. That's also the biggest obstacle to legacy giving," he says. "The sooner-is-better, cash-based mindset of a capital campaign is exactly the opposite of what is needed with legacy giving."

But the differences between the two don't mean they can't complement each other. Johnson offers the following suggestions for successfully incorporating planned giving into capital campaigns.

1. **Start a planned giving campaign before your capital campaign.** Planned gifts are often pursued in the waning months of a capital campaign, which Johnson thinks is the worst possible time. "Legacy gifts involve conversations about values and vision. Those are conversations you want to have before you approach someone in a capital campaign. If you've already established a match in values, the question donors will be asking won't be whether to give in support of capital projects, but how much to give."

2. **Watch the language used in soliciting legacy gifts.** When planned giving is mentioned in capital campaign solicitations, the language used often makes it seem like a secondary or optional gift, says Johnson. "Gift officers need to make sure legacy giving doesn't feel like a second-class

conversation to donors," he says. "You definitely need to avoid any sense of, 'Gee, since you're too much of a loser to give a big gift now, how about a planned gift in the future?'"

3. **Relate legacy giving to immediate capital needs.** Giving legacy conversations as much weight as cash conversations is difficult if planned giving is not directly related to campaign goals, says Johnson. Making these concrete and tangible connections — providing funded depreciation for a building under construction, for example, or establishing an endowment to pay a program's future staff — will increase the likelihood of receiving planned gifts, he says.

4. **Keep systems of counting gifts clear — and separate.** "Counting gifts for the balance sheet is different from counting gifts for fundraising objectives, and mixing the two almost always does a disservice to the organization," says Johnson. "You should be tracking whatever metrics are most relevant to the fundraising goals you've adopted. Don't let the auditing/accounting conversation be your only source of metrics."

5. **Keep things (including terminology) simple.** The phrase planned gifts has, in Johnson's opinion, come to represent a set of dauntingly complex giving instruments in donors' minds. Because of this — and because 90 to 95 percent of all planned gift dollars come from simple bequests — he prefers the term legacy giving to planned giving. He also advocates framing donor expectations by focusing on the impact and values of gifts, rather than the mechanics of realizing them.

Source: Kevin Johnson, Principal, Retriever Development Counsel, LLC, Portland, OR. E-mail: kevin@retrieverdevelopment.com

Setting the Size, Scope and Campaign Duration

Endowment Vs. Capital Campaigns: Why the Difference Matters

Capital campaigns have long been a feature of the major fundraising landscape. Comprehensive campaigns have become an increasingly popular way to provide both bricks-and-mortar facilities and program/upkeep revenue. But endowment campaigns, less common though they might be, are just as important, says Larry Karnoff, director of planned giving at Feeding America (Chicago, IL).

Here Karnoff compares endowment campaigns with traditional capital campaigns, and discusses how nonprofits can make the most of them.

What is the fundamental difference between capital campaigns and endowment campaigns?

"Capital campaigns generally have a short-term goal, maybe five years or so, and have a very clear aim — to build this building or renovate those facilities. Endowment campaigns have a much longer time horizon and are more focused on underwriting the general operations of an organization and enhancing its creditworthiness."

How do the types of messaging used in the two campaigns differ?

"Pure capital campaigns are rare these days, and comprehensive campaigns basically ask everyone for everything. Endowment campaigns usually focus on one of two basic messages. The first centers on economic uncertainty: 'For us to remain viable in the long term, we need to have a rainy-day fund of secure investments, and our current endowment isn't big enough to handle another downturn.' The second focuses on ongoing development: 'This is our vision of growth, and to underwrite that growth far into the future, we need a larger endowment.'"

What kind of prospects should be the focus of endowment campaigns?

"People with long-term commitment to the organization, probably insiders like board members, senior administrators and major gift donors. Endowment campaigns aren't talking about specific programs themselves, they're talking about the underlying financial foundation of the organization. And a prospect should already be knowledgeable and committed to an organization's mission before being invited into a conversation about its financial security. That's an insider conversation."

What kinds of gifts should an endowment campaign be seeking?

"Planned gifts and bequests can be the basis of endowment campaigns, for two reasons. One is that they are a long-term income stream that fits well with the long-term horizon of endowments. But relying on planned gifts also develops within the institution the competency to build a comprehensive fundraising program which includes these vehicles. Not only is it good for long-term growth, it's also good for the immediate development of the advancement department."

How does marketing differ between endowment and capital campaigns?

"Endowment campaigns will typically not have as large a marketing component as capital campaigns. The endowment campaign's justification and goal will be announced to the public in public forums, but solicitation should be directed toward major gift prospects. The capital campaign public phase seeking small donations from numerous supporters isn't usually needed in endowment campaigns."

How would a nonprofit go about planning a first endowment campaign?

"I believe the process should start with the chief development officer sitting down with the chief financial officer and having a long talk about the organization's development, investment and long-term growth. From this conversation would come a dollar amount of what it would take to fund the organization's vision of the future for the next, say, 20 years. The development officer's role then would be to translate that conversation into a case that can be presented to donors."

Source: Larry Karnoff, Director of Planned Giving, Feeding America, Chicago, IL. E-mail: Lkarnoff@feedingamerica.org

---

Pre-campaign Tip

All charities impact the economic development, cultural, educational and community development components of a community. Knowing the extent of this impact can be used to develop the marketing and positioning strategy of your capital campaign.

PRE-CAMPAIGN

Setting the Size, Scope and Campaign Duration

Assign Target Dates for Generated Gift Revenue

There's nothing worse than getting to the final quarter of a capital campaign and realizing far less money has been raised than necessary to meet the goal. It's equally disheartening for a development officer to hit the midyear mark knowing less than 40 percent of his/her yearly fundraising goal has been raised.

To better anticipate what needs to be done by when, develop a timetable whenever there's a fundraising goal to be met. Break it down into monthly and/or quarterly projections, and put the greatest pressure on the front end of your calendar, knowing how it traditionally becomes more challenging to raise additional funds as you approach the final months. If you can set yourself up to meet your goal earlier in the year, anything else you are able to generate becomes extra.

By projecting the amount of funds to be raised at monthly intervals — and placing more emphasis at the front end of your cycle — you can better monitor if you are on track as each month progresses.

	Projected Fundraising Target										
Total Campaign Goal: $5 million											
Development Officer_____											
Individual Yearly Goal_____											
Jul	Aug	Sept	Oct	Nov	Dec	Jan	Feb	Mar	Apr	May	June
0	50M	50M	200M	300M	300M	100M	100M	50M	50M	0	0

Give Thought to Your Campaign Slogan

In planning and executing your next campaign, it's important to give a great deal of thought to the slogan you plan to use throughout its duration.

Will the use of the funds be singular or multipurpose? Who will be your audience? Is the campaign running separate from other fundraising efforts or will it include your annual fund gifts and, perhaps, planned gift provisions? Are you seeking major gifts only from a smaller constituency, or will you approach all who are interested, regardless of gift size?

Are you seeking funds for bricks and mortar or programs?

How does timing fit into your campaign — are you celebrating an anniversary, will the campaign go into the next century or be tied to a previous fundraising effort?

The answers to these and other questions will help to provide the basis for a slogan that will be 1) appropriate for your campaign, 2) impressionable and 3) lasting.

Here are some slogans — both new and used — to consider as you formulate one that best fits your organization's own circumstances:

- Bridge to Distinction
- Foundation for the Second Century
- Building a Legacy of Love
- To Benefit Those Who Follow
- Hope for Tomorrow
- That Others Might Grow
- Leading the Way
- Decade for Growth
- Shared Vision for the Future

- Now More Than Ever
- Because We Care
- Bringing Strength to Our Future
- Pathway to Achievement
- Nurturing a New Generation
- Sustaining Our Commitment
- To Serve Those in Need
- To Build an Impregnable Future
- Building a Better Tomorrow
- Illuminating Our Future
- Design for the Next Decade

Perhaps these slogans can provide the needed "fodder" to develop your own message.

Successful Capital Campaigns: From Start to Finish, Third Edition.
Edited by Scott C. Stevenson.
© 2012 Stevenson, Inc. Published 2012 by Stevenson, Inc.

Successful Capital Campaigns: From Start to Finish — 3ʳᵈ Edition

PRE-CAMPAIGN

Bringing Structure and Organization to Your Effort

Although ownership of your capital campaign should have taken root early in the planning process, this is where the rubber begins to meet the road. First and foremost, your board needs to fully understand and accept their individual and collective responsibility for giving and getting. The leadership role they assume will set the bar for gifts that follow as well as the willingness and enthusiasm of others to serve in various volunteer capacities.

The Board's Role Will Impact Campaign Success

Although the success of a capital campaign is dependent on a number of factors, the role your board plays will be a key factor in determining its ultimate success.

To begin, board leadership makes a campaign possible. It gives the campaign legitimacy. It allows you to make solicitation approaches. It represents a call to the community to make extraordinary commitments of time and money. It allows you to say, "The board has authorized...."

Campaigns represent "organisms" that will change your organization like a storm gathering energy. That's why it's so important for your board to recognize the opportunity a campaign presents to transform a vision into reality. Your board needs to understand that, if they don't love you, no one else will. Your board needs to give 100 percent, in terms of time, financial resources and enthusiasm.

Board members should provide the nucleus fund of campaign gifts that come before lead gifts. Capital campaigns should be run top down and inside out, meaning board support comes first. And since your board members should be key solicitors throughout the campaign, it's important for them to recognize that sacrificial donors (those whose gifts represent real sacrifice) become the best solicitors.

Key board members must model the leadership needed in order to convince other board members of the campaign's importance. Ask yourself, "Who on my board do people really follow?"

Knowing board support can account for as much as 30 to 60 percent of a campaign goal, it's important that you recruit members who have the ability to make significant gifts. It's equally important that they know the paramount role they hold in your campaign's success.

Share Expectations With Your Campaign Chair

A time expectations summary can be an important tool in recruiting the most able and influential person to chair your campaign. Sharing time expectations with your potential chair in advance of his/her acceptance of the position accomplishes three key objectives:

1. Demonstrates that you are highly organized, an important trait for a would-be volunteer to know in deciding whether to accept the job.

2. Spells out expectations for the chairperson up front so he/she can make an informed decision about accepting the position.

3. Helps to prepare your potential chairperson to hit the ground running if he/she is given a clear picture of his/her role in your upcoming campaign.

Use this example to create a time expectations chart for your campaign chair:

TIME EXPECTATIONS FOR CAPITAL CAMPAIGN CHAIRPERSON		
ACTION	**MONTH**	**NO. OF MTGS**
Meeting w/staff for campaign planning	January '12	2
Recruit co-chairs for Lead Gifts: Individuals, Corporations/ Businesses and Foundations Committees	February	
Orientation Meeting w/Co-chairs	March	1
Orientation Meeting w/all committees	April	1
Decision on Your Campaign Commitment	April	
Solicitation w/staff of Co-chairs	April	
Attend Lead Gifts committees as needed	May - July	3 - 6
Conduct final report meeting at end of lead gift phase	August	
Public phase planning meeting w/staff	September	2
Recruit public phase committee chairs: Individuals, Corporations/Businesses	September	
Orientation Meeting w/all committees	October	1
Public announcement event	October	1
Attend committee meetings as needed	Oct. '12-June '14	3-9
Review meeting w/staff	January	1
Review meeting w/staff	May	1
Press Conference	May	1
Post-campaign Celebration	July	1
Post Campaign Meeting	July	1

Bringing Structure and Organization to Your Effort

Campaign Leadership: Why Have Honorary Chairs?

How might an honorary chair or co-chairs — especially when they're also well-regarded celebrities — make a noticeable difference in a capital campaign's success? We spoke with Nancy Petruso, associate vice chancellor and chief of staff at Texas Christian University (Fort Worth, TX), which will soon be wrapping up a four-year capital campaign. Former "CBS Evening News" anchor and "60 Minutes" correspondent Bob Schieffer and his wife have served as honorary co-chairs of the campaign.

How did you go about approaching the Schieffers to take on the roles of honorary co-chairs?

"They're both TCU alumni and Mrs. Schieffer is a member of the board of trustees. Both of them have been very involved as volunteers with TCU for a long time. Our school of journalism here at TCU was named for Mr. Schieffer about four years ago, so it just seemed like a very logical thing to do, to extend that invitation to them."

How does having honorary chairs make a notable difference in the campaign's success?

"I don't know how you would really go about measuring the impact that it has. But I think having somebody in that position, well-known to the broadest number of our alumni and friends and parents, lends a lot of credence to the validity of the campaign. I think it helps if you have someone of that stature endorsing it."

Are there any specific duties or expectations that you had of them as honorary chairs?

"The only thing that we specifically said we would like them to do was to be present at our public kickoff event, which took place back in April of 2008. Mr. Schieffer served as master of ceremonies for that event. And then any celebration event that

we have at the conclusion of the campaign in May of this year."

Were there any concerns that the Schieffers had before assuming their roles that you needed to address?

"Not that I'm aware of. I wasn't involved personally in their recruitment, but I'm fairly certain that there were no major concerns that they had."

What does staff do behind the scenes to support the efforts of your honorary chairs?

"Our vice chancellor is really their primary contact and the go-between with our fundraising staff here on campus. And of course, our donor relations staff was very involved with the planning of the kickoff event. They were charged with getting them to the right place at the right time on the day of the kickoff and making sure that all of that was coordinated."

Can you point to any examples of how having honorary chairs helped to bring about major gifts that otherwise might not have happened?

"I can't cite any specific examples. I don't believe that they have been directly involved with the solicitation of any gifts, although there may have been some discussions. Mrs. Schieffer is a member of the board of trustees, so she may have had discussions with other members."

At what point, and in what way, did you solicit your honorary chairs for a major gift?

"There are always ongoing discussions with them by the chancellor and vice chancellor. That's just sort of an annual thing."

Source: Nancy Petruso, Associate Vice Chancellor and Chief of Staff, Texas Christian University, Office of University Advancement, Fort Worth, TX. E-mail: n.petruso@tcu.edu

Why an Honorary Campaign Committee Makes Good Sense

Although your upcoming capital campaign should include a working steering committee, it makes good sense to enlist an honorary committee as well. Why? Even though these individuals may not be expected to give of their time like those on a steering committee, this group of financially capable, highly respected individuals serves a broader purpose:

1. The fact that they have agreed to be a part of this august group serves to engage them as more likely major donors to your effort. They will be among your initial lead gift calls.

2. Their reputations add substance and credibility to your campaign. Depending on the type of organization you represent, the group's make up may be national in scope.

3. Although their time commitment to the campaign will be far less than that of steering committee members, there may be instances in which they would be willing to make

introductions with peers, host an event or even accompany you on calls.

By virtue of their association with the campaign, these committee members want to see the campaign succeed. Serving on this committee makes it less likely that they would distance themselves from your effort prior to its successful completion

Consider Campaign Co-chairs

Many campaigns have more than one chairperson. Sharing the responsibility allows twice as much contributed time, leadership and potential for top-level giving. As you consider co-chair combinations, give thought to a parent-child combination, particularly with a family whose giving capacity merits a long and continuing relationship with your organization.

PRE-CAMPAIGN   Bringing Structure and Organization to Your Effort

Advice on Enlisting Campaign Leadership

Gearing up for a major fundraising effort that will require competent and committed volunteer leadership? Look for these key qualities in persons you hope to recruit:

- Those whose level of gift support will be exemplary to others.
- Those who are widely known and respected.

- Those who have had fundraising experience as volunteers or board members.
- Those who have had past involvement with your organization.
- Those who are dependable and maintain a can-do attitude.
- Those with demonstrated management and organizational skills.

How to Train Your Campaign's Volunteer Leaders

The 24-person campaign leadership committee for Colorado State University (Fort Collins, CO) includes persons who have taken a significant lead in the university's campaign and who have made or who are in the process of making a significant gift.

Members all receive a job description and 155-page campaign volunteer guide (see box right) containing information they need to be successful in soliciting gifts for the campaign, says Susan Latimer, executive director of principal and planned giving.

"As part of our committee member enlistment process, we made sure that their role was very clear and that everyone on the committee agreed to their role," Latimer says. "Each committee member is armed with solid information so that they can effectively articulate the case for giving to Colorado State."

At the first training session, committee members received job descriptions and the campaign volunteer guide and were asked what else they needed, says Latimer: "They said they needed an elevator speech, so we developed one for them."

Donors and other volunteers who have been successful in soliciting gifts also conduct peer-to-peer training with committee members.

Committee members meet twice per year formally and individually to support their volunteer efforts. They are also invited to a wide variety of other events, including the Green and Gold Gala and the 1870 Dinner (a major donor dinner).

Content not available in this edition

Committee members receive a monthly newsletter detailing the campaign's progress and gifts brought in to date. "I try to call or meet with everyone on the committee at least three times per year," says Latimer. "I want to be sure to enable them to be successful by giving them as many tools as possible."

Source: Susan Latimer, Executive Director of Principal & Planned Giving, Colorado State University, Fort Collins, CO.
E-mail: slatimer@ua.colostate.edu

Bringing Structure and Organization to Your Effort

Keep Your Steering Committee Motivated

Capital campaigns can be energizing and draining. They can become particularly draining at some point following the public announcement phase when pledges drop off and it appears difficult to garner additional support.

Your steering committee's ability to stay energized will impact ultimate campaign success. To keep this important group motivated:

✓ **Plan meeting agendas.** Meet with the committee chair prior to each meeting to identify next steps. Doing so will instill greater confidence among steering committee members.

✓ **Celebrate victories.** Be sure to point out key accomplishments that have been made since the group met last.

✓ **Keep members focused on tasks at hand.** Work from your agenda and follow up assignments with individual memos confirming assignments.

✓ **Consult with fundraising counsel.** Assuming you have secured an established fundraising consultant, turn to him/her to be sure you're not missing any strategies to meet your campaign goal.

Strengthen Board Member Solicitation Skills

Board member solicitation can make or break fundraising efforts for one simple reason, says Jim Lyons, senior partner at Pride Philanthropy (Alpharetta, GA): Board members are five to 10 times more likely to get appointments with potential donors than development staff.

"It's easy to turn down a professional fundraiser; their job is to get turned down," Lyons says. "But when a volunteer who is giving their own money to an organization calls and says 'This is really important, and I'd like to tell you about it,' people will usually make time to listen."

Lyons answers questions about creating effective board member solicitors:

What is the biggest obstacle to effective board member fundraising?

"It often goes back to how they were recruited. All too often we are so focused on recruiting toward yes that we end up down-playing critical fundraising expectations. It gets us board members, but it sets our organizations up for failure."

How should fundraising expectations be communicated to potential or new board members?

"They need to be told there are different ways to help. Some people are good at identifying prospects, some are good at telling an organization's story, and some don't want to set up appointments or take hard questions, but are willing to look someone in the eye and make the ask. No one has to do all three, but all board members should know that they are expected to be contributing in at least one area."

How should development staff assist board member solicitation?

"They should first of all help board members develop a prospect list of three to five contacts. (Any more will look like a job and the board member won't do it.) They should prepare the meeting materials, should expect to do much of the follow up, and can,

according to the board member's preference, attend meetings to answer detail questions and supply statistics. But they should never set up the meeting. If a staff member calls to make an appointment on someone's behalf, it defeats the whole purpose."

What should board members know about closing solicitations?

"There are three keys. First, make sure you always ask for a specific amount. When you offer a range, people will always migrate to the bottom end. Second, when you have made the ask, just be quiet. It can be hard to sit through the silence, but if you start talking, you'll often be talking them out of the gift. Last, make sure there is a specific follow-up plan that leaves the ball in your court — something like 'I understand this is a big decision. Tell me when you would like us to follow up with you.'"

What should be included in training to build board members' solicitation skills?

"It's nice to have a meeting strictly devoted to solicitation training. You will want to do some role play and practice in the meeting — pair everyone up so they are not performing in front of each other, but have each member play both the solicitor and the donor. People will resist, but they always say it was helpful after the fact."

How do you establish an ongoing culture of board member fundraising?

"It starts at the top. It needs to be an ongoing CEO message and an important part of board member orientation and training. It's a process that takes time. You can't just send a memo and say you've established a culture of philanthropy. It requires long-term commitment."

Source: Jim Lyons, Senior Partner, Pride Philanthropy, Alpharetta, GA. E-mail: Prideljim@aol.com

Bringing Structure and Organization to Your Effort

Solicitation Team Should Be Prepared

It's not uncommon to have two, three or sometimes four individuals involved in a major gift solicitation. When that's the case, it's important that each team member be well-prepared for the solicitation.

The appropriate number of solicitors will be determined, in part, by the number of prospects being called upon by them. It's not uncommon, for instance, to have a team of two solicitors present with a husband and wife. If the couple has a child or financial advisor present as well, you may get by with a third or perhaps fourth member on your solicitation team. It's important to remember, however, not to overpower the prospect(s) with too many solicitors.

Planning and preparation are key elements in the successful major gift solicitation. As the development officer, it's your job to see that those involved in the solicitation of a major gift are well versed on every aspect of the call, including:

- **The project.** Team members should have an adequate understanding of the project to be funded. Can everyone involved articulate the project's importance to the donor, to his/her family, or to the community? At least one team member should be able to address technical project questions, and others on the team should know to direct questions to that person.
- **The written proposal (if there is one).** Each solicitation team member should have reviewed the proposal

thoroughly prior to the visit and addressed any points that may not be clear. Additionally, team members should understand the project budget. Finally, be sure that every proposal has an executive summary. Some prospects will not take the time to study an entire proposal, so the executive summary should be able to stand on its own if the prospect reads nothing else.

- **The prospect.** Familiarize team members with the prospect and pertinent actions that have taken place in the cultivation/solicitation process. Do team members have an adequate understanding of the prospect's personality? Likes and dislikes? Are there any topics that should be avoided during the conversation? Answers to these and other questions will provide a smoother flow throughout the meeting.
- **Each participants's role in the major gift solicitation.** Who will ultimately ask for the gift? Do other team members know when to step into the conversation (or refrain from speaking)? Who will take the lead in describing the project? It's important to have both the timing and the delivery of the solicitation well thought out in advance of the meeting. If you want only the prospect to speak after the ask, then let team members know that in advance.

Hold a Briefing Meeting for Your Solicitation Team

There's nothing worse than watching a nervous person make a speech — except, perhaps, watching a nervous person make a solicitation, says David Phillips, president and CEO of Custom Development Solutions, Inc. (Mt. Pleasant, SC).

"Stammering, stuttering and apologizing are a disaster in the making," Phillips says. "You need a solicitor who will unashamedly look a donor in the face and calmly, clearly and articulately ask for their support. And you get that by making sure people feel well-rehearsed and well-prepared."

To achieve such preparation, Phillips advocates convening a formal meeting of all solicitors (he recommends at least two), plus any related development officers and outside fundraising counsel. The aim of the meeting is to choreograph, point by point, what issues will be stressed, in what order, and by whom. Deciding who will make the ask is central, but Phillips says to also put thought into how you will introduce and position the request.

The briefing can serve different purposes with different personnel, says Phillips. For teams with less-experienced members, it presents an opportunity to assess capacity and give extra coaching. For long-standing teams, it creates a space for brainstorming and focused review of project details and prospect history and information.

A natural companion to the briefing meeting is a formal debriefing held as soon as possible after the call, says Phillips. Considering questions like how the call went, whether the request was made properly, what can be done to effect the most positive response and what upcoming action steps will provide a mechanism to establish ongoing learning and continuous improvement.

Source: David Phillips, President and CEO, Custom Development Solutions, Inc., Mt. Pleasant, SC. E-mail: dgp@cdsfunds.com

---

Focus Preparation on Four Possible Solicitation Replies

Inexperienced development officers often agonize over problematic solicitation scenarios. To lessen that anxiety, explain that virtually all responses fall into four categories, says David Phillips, president and CEO of Custom Development Solutions, Inc. (Mt. Pleasant, SC):

"A prospect can say, 'Yes,' and you start talking details. A prospect can say, 'No, it's not for me,' and that is pretty much that. A prospect can say, 'Wow, that's a significant commitment. I'll need some time to think about it.' This is the most common response and mostly just needs a follow-up meeting.

"Finally, a prospect can say something like, 'I can't do $100,000, but I might be able to do $50,000.' This is the most complicated response, because you then need to figure out whether you will accept that amount or suggest a higher figure."

Phillips says that figuring out which category any given scenario falls into can help volunteers or new solicitors feel more comfortable and prepared.

Bringing Structure and Organization to Your Effort

Weekly Reports Keep Committee Members Engaged, Motivated

To keep capital campaign committee members engaged and motivated, Andrew Takami, executive director of development, Ivy Tech Community College Southern Indiana (Sellersburg, IN), e-mails a weekly report of fundraising activities by 8 a.m. each Monday.

The e-mail subject line for each report follows a consistent format: "Weekly Report #(0) for the week ending (day, month, date)" so that it is easily recognizable by recipients, says Takami. Each weekly report includes:

✓ Fundraising activities for the previous week.

✓ Specific funds brought in.

✓ Activities for the upcoming week.

✓ The list of people with whom volunteers and staff met.

✓ A list of speaking engagements that occurred.

✓ A list of events that were held.

✓ A list of donors to the campaign to date.

✓ The grand total of all donations made to the campaign to date.

✓ The dates of upcoming committee meetings.

This simple communications tool helps keep everyone engaged and on track, says Takami. "People are busy," he says. "Because the weekly reports contain all the information they need, all they have to do is go to this once-a-week e-mail to keep up to date."

Source: Andrew Takami, Executive Director of Development, Ivy Tech Community College, Southern Indiana, Sellersburg, IN. E-mail: atakami@ivytech.edu

The director of development for Ivy Tech Community College, Southern Indiana (Sellersburg, IN), e-mails this report to capital campaign committee members first thing every Monday.

Content not available in this edition

Time Foundation Proposals

If you're about to embark on a capital campaign and hope to secure foundation grants as part of that goal, it's important to:

1. Include only those foundations with a history of participating in capital campaigns among your list of prospects.

2. Know the best time to approach each foundation during your campaign cycle. For instance, some foundations are known for making challenge grants at the front end of a campaign while others may prefer to make a challenge gift during the latter part of the effort, as a way to help generate the final gifts needed to make goal. Other foundations' decisions to give are based, in part, on who, how many and what percentage of your constituency have supported the campaign to date.

Successful Capital Campaigns: From Start to Finish, Third Edition.
Edited by Scott C. Stevenson.
© 2012 Stevenson, Inc. Published 2012 by Stevenson, Inc.

Successful Capital Campaigns: From Start to Finish — 3rd Edition

The Quiet (Lead Gift) Phase

This is a crucial point in the success of your campaign. The point at which you and others seek lead gifts — the quiet or unannounced phase of your capital campaign — will determine the size, scope and ultimate success of your effort. The gifts solicited during this phase should account for no less than 40 to 60 percent of your overall campaign goal. These gifts will originate from your most financially-capable, not necessarily your most committed, donors. It's not unusual that the major gifts derived from this portion of your campaign actually come more easily than the smaller gifts that materialize during the public phase of your campaign. Then again, more planning should go into the cultivation and approach taken with each of these donors.

Structure Your Campaign to Maximize Quiet Phase Fundraising

Perhaps no part of a capital campaign is as important as its quiet phase. Not only does this period generate a significant portion of the overall goal, if not an outright majority, the philanthropic leadership it establishes fuels the public appeal that follows.

Quiet-phase fundraising has been central to the capital campaign underway at the Ronald McDonald House of Fort Worth, TX, says Capital Campaign Director Angie Gallaway. She says that in their case, it lasted about a year: A feasibility study was conducted in July 2010, officials began soliciting leadership gifts in August 2010, and the public portion of the campaign was announced in August 2011.

How was this timeline determined? "We definitely wanted to raise at least half the overall goal during the quiet phase," says Gallaway, noting that $4.8 million of the $8 million goal had been secured when the announcement was made. But this wasn't the only consideration. "We also applied to a large foundation for funding for a challenge grant. So we waited until we had that response, so we could publicize that challenge to the public."

The organization's supporters are many, but officials focused quiet fundraising efforts on a few key constituent groups. These included major local foundations, local corporations with close ties to the nonprofit, supporters of past capital campaigns, and the organization's major gifts donors. Total calls, including those with board members, numbered around 65.

Gallaway says that a large percentage of quiet gifts came in the first few months, with a few coming as early as during the initial feasibility visits. She says that currently, with the public phase of the campaign now ongoing, officials are still working with a few major donors, but that focus has shifted to reaching out to contacts of the campaign steering committee and board of directors.

With the public campaign in full swing, Gallaway says a major goal is now making the most of the leadership gifts given during the quiet phase. Steps she is taking in that regard include:

- Working with local newspapers and business press to create a foldout insert highlighting the campaign, the donations it has received and the support it still needs.
- Listing all naming opportunities in campaign brochures and showing which are already reserved. "Seeing who else has given and at what level is encouraging for some prospects," says Gallaway.
- Mentioning the leadership gifts already received at all cultivation events and facility tours.
- Including in all solicitation proposals an up-to-date list of gifts and pledges received, as well as a list of all major donors.

Source: Angie Gallaway, Capital Campaign Director, Ronald McDonald House of Fort Worth, Fort Worth, TX.
E-mail: Angie.Gallaway@ftworthrmh.org

One Board Member Needs to Set the Precedent

You can have a who's who of individuals serving on your board of trustees. However, until one member steps forward with an unprecedented, sacrificial gift, others may very well refrain from giving at highly capable levels.

Work at convincing that most-capable board member of his/her role before other board members step up to the plate with less-than-desirable pledges. Help that single board member realize the potential he/she possesses. Paint a picture of what could be versus what's probable without his/her level of leadership.

Your shared vision should depict specific examples of how your organization will achieve greatness with a great gift.

Factors That Impact Campaign Success

It's not even debatable. Your nonprofit's CEO must not only be willing to make key solicitation calls, she/he must do it with enthusiasm. A CEO who procrastinates or avoids cultivation and solicitation responsibilities will ultimately contribute to a failed campaign.

PRE-CAMPAIGN   The Quiet (Lead Gift) Phase

Develop Solicitation Strategies for Top Prospects

You have identified a prospect you believe capable of giving $200,000 to your cause. You have introduced her to your organization, properly cultivated her and are approaching the point in the solicitation cycle of closing the gift.

How can you best plan for a successful solicitation? Who should make the ask? Who should be present? What needs to happen to ensure success?

When nearing the closing phase of a major gift request, it's wise to formulate your solicitation strategy.

Based on what you know about the prospect, first meet with key staff to outline a potential strategy and determine who should be involved in the solicitation. Then, invite those persons you deem most appropriate for the solicitation team and request their input as you share your solicitation outline.

This process of shaping an intended solicitation strategy with staff and then seeking volunteer input allows your volunteers to further shape an already sound plan. And by inviting their input, you engage them in owning the solicitation process.

Strategy meetings should cover topics including:

- Prospect's rating (as a major gift donor).
- Who, how and when to best set the appointment.
- Preferred time and location.
- Others who may be present or should be invited.
- Asking amount.
- Giving gap — amount the prospect may have in mind versus the intended ask amount.
- Strategies to close the giving gap.
- Presentation format — who says what and when.
- Uses of the gift.
- Benefits to donor.
- Materials to be shared at meeting and/or sent in advance.
- Potential outcomes and responses/follow-up of the request.

While this process may seem a bit daunting, rest assured, the more you use it, the easier and more natural it will become. Do so knowing that your degree of success will be enhanced significantly by making this a regular exercise.

SOLICITATION STRATEGY WORKSHEET

Today's Date:_____

Scheduled Solicitation Date _____   Location _____

Prospect(s) _____

Rating _____

Home Ph_____   Business Ph_____

E-mail _____   Cell _____

Ask Amount *(given over time)* $_____

Giving Gap *(amount the donor has in mind)* $_____

Possible Uses of Gift *(in order of priority)*
1._____
2._____
3._____
4._____

Perceived Benefits for the Donor
1._____
2._____
3._____
4._____

Solicitor Team *(Preferably limited to three persons)*
Assigned Staff
1._____
2._____
3._____
Assigned Volunteer(s)
1._____
2._____
3._____

Additional Invitees/Attendees of Prospect
1._____
2._____
3._____

Materials Needed for Meeting
_____ ❑ Send in Advance ❑ Share at Meeting
_____ ❑ Send in Advance ❑ Share at Meeting
_____ ❑ Send in Advance ❑ Share at Meeting

Preferred Presentation Format *(who says what)*
Conversation Leader: _____
Solicitor: _____
Support:_____

Potential Outcomes
Outcome #1 _____
Response/Follow-up _____

Outcome #2 _____
Response/Follow-up _____

Outcome #3 _____
Response/Follow-up _____

Scale of Gifts Helps During Closing Process

Textbook solicitation suggests that you should ask each donor for a specific gift amount when making the ask. That's true. But, there are times, for any number of legitimate reasons, where that may not be the wisest move.

In instances in which you don't feel it's right to ask for a specific amount, here's another useful approach you can take. Have a scale-of-giving chart at your disposal when it comes time for making the ask. Pull out the chart and, if you choose, use a colored marker to highlight a particular gift range or draw a circle around that portion of the gift range that you hope the prospect will come in at with a gift and then pose this question: "Where do you see yourself giving within the area I've highlighted?"

This useful method allows you to set a minimum gift level without pinpointing an exact amount.

VISIONS MADE REAL
CAMPAIGN

Goal: $8 million

Scale of Gifts Required to Achieve Goal

Gift Range	Gifts Required	Total
$1 million or more	2	$2,000,000
$500,000 to 999,000	4	$2,000,000
$250,000 to 499,000	6	$1,500,000
$100,000 to 249,000	10	$1,000,000
$50,000 to 99,000	15	$750,000
$25,000 to 49,000	20	$500,000
$10,000 to 24,000	20	$200,000
Less than $10,000	500	$50,000
		$8,000,000

Anatomy of a Major Lead Gift

Executive Director Milton Key, Presbyterian Communities and Services Foundation (Dallas, TX) says a lead gift of $18.4 million from T. Boone Pickens was the result of a couple of streams that led into a river.

"Within 12 months a staff member from the T. Boone Pickens Foundation put her mom in one of our care centers, enabling her to experience our quality of care, while at the same time, one of our board members was able to arrange an opportunity for the CEO of Presbyterian Communities and Services to meet with Mr. Pickens."

The result was a transformational naming gift from Pickens, which will aid in the building of the T. Boone Pickens Hospice and Palliative Care Center — the first community-based inpatient hospice care center in Dallas — offering world-class, comprehensive end-of-life care.

Key said the gift was unique to them, in the sense that they were asking someone to support something that doesn't exist yet. "We had an opportunity to present our vision to his

foundation, but that's it. We didn't have blueprints, just a plan for what we hoped to accomplish." Pickens, who is known as a risk taker, had made similar leaps of faith in the past.

Moving forward, Key says that the Pickens Foundation is aware of and very willing to help Key leverage the gift. "Since Mr. Pickens is on board with this gift, people want to know what's so great about the hospice center. It gives us an opportunity to let people know what we do."

In the end, Key says that kind of relationship building is what made this gift possible in the first place. "You need to be aware of the opportunities you have to meet other people, for example through existing board members, and be proactive in learning what their interests are and how that might be connected to what you do."

Source: Milton Key, Executive Director, Presbyterian Communities and Services Foundation, Dallas, TX. E-mail: mkey@prescs.org

Encourage Restricted Gifts to Supercharge Your Fundraising

Imagine a university launching a capital campaign to build a new science facility. Now imagine that same campaign if officials refused to disclose what the donations would be used to support.

Ludicrous as the idea of making million-dollar appeals in an information vacuum sounds, Penelope Burk, president of Cygnus Applied Research, (Chicago, IL), says nonprofits are doing something very similar every single day. "Unrestricted solicitations are guaranteed — guaranteed! — to raise less money than solicitations in which the donor is told what the money will support. But boards and CEOs insist on unrestricted funds."

The problem with unrestricted fundraising, Burk says, is one of cultivation and stewardship. "The best way to inspire donor loyalty is to report the concrete effects donations had on specific programs. This connects donors with the organization and inclines them toward further, larger gifts. But if the initial gift was unrestricted, you have nothing to talk about except the worthiness of the organization as a whole."

In this situation gift officers end up selling the organizational brand over and over, which Burk says works fine the first time, but not so well after that. "Once donors give a gift, they become investors in the organization, and as investors they are interested in the return on their investment, on the real-world impact they are having. And if you can't or don't provide that concrete feedback, they drift away."

An unrestricted approach also complicates the solicitation process, she says. "If you ask for money but can't tie it to a specific program or service, donors tend to conclude that either A. You don't have any sort of long-term strategy; or B. You don't really know why you're asking and, therefore, don't need the money."

Burk's answer is to get rid of unrestricted giving entirely. "CFOs will say it's impossible, but it's actually quite simple," she says.

Most objections stem from fundamental misconceptions about budgeting programs and services, she explains. "Most not-for-profit budgets are identical to for-profit budgets — salaries, benefits, office supplies and so on. What nonprofits need to do is

move to cost-centered budgeting where all expenditures are attributed to programs and service delivery."

In this arrangement, every program's budget would include not only its direct costs, but also the salaries of staff needed to manage it, a portion of the CEO's salary and a portion of all fixed costs such as physical facilities and utilities. "Nothing is left over in a cost-centered budget," says Burk. "There is no administrative overhead, so all gifts will be supporting mission-critical programming."

Burk says an all-assigned fundraising approach — she prefers the terms "assigned" or "designated" to "restricted" — needs effective case statements and requires discipline in setting solicitation priorities. But she says such a system is a great boon for gift officers.

"It really lets them out of a straight jacket," she says. "If every gift officer were allowed to adopt an all-assigned model this morning, every not-for-profit would be raising far more money this afternoon."

Source: Penelope Burk, President, Cygnus Applied Research, Chicago, IL. E-mail: Penelope.burk@cygresearch.com

> ### Unrestricted Giving: Will Donors Run Wild?
>
> CEOs and boards of directors often worry that allowing donors to make restricted gifts will open a Pandora's box of trouble, with donors running amuck through the organization and development officers struggling to pay the bills that need to be paid.
>
> That concern is unfounded, says Penelope Burk, president of Cygnus Applied Research, (Chicago, IL). "The only thing you should be selling are the programs you want your donors to support. And donors will almost always support the strategic priorities that you set, provided you sell them in a convincing, compelling and logical way," she says.
>
> "You are the experts and donors will rarely second-guess you. Just make sure you are clear in articulating your case to them."

Promote the Triple Gift in Capital Campaigns

Capital campaigns are a great way to encourage over-and-above giving. One way to promote this holistic kind of thinking without sacrificing ongoing annual support is to promote the triple gift.

The triple gift is exactly what it sounds like, a three-part solicitation seeking a mid-level gift for the annual fund, a larger gift for the goal of the campaign — whether it be for endowment

or capital — and a planned gift for the long-term stability of the organization.

This might sound like a lot to ask of supporters, but presented together, the three gifts offer a coherent and complementary vision of support that can be surprisingly easy to "sell" to committed donors. Of the three, planned giving will likely be the most unfamiliar, so make sure you have collateral material that effectively explains its operation and benefits.

Successful Capital Campaigns: From Start to Finish, Third Edition.
Edited by Scott C. Stevenson.
© 2012 Stevenson, Inc. Published 2012 by Stevenson, Inc.

Successful Capital Campaigns: From Start to Finish — 3rd Edition

CAMPAIGN

Publicly Announcing Your Campaign... With Enthusiasm

The public announcement of your capital campaign follows the quiet phase. At this time, 50 percent or more of your campaign goal should be committed. The public announcement serves to inform those who have yet to make a contribution about your campaign and begins the final solicitation phase which includes larger numbers of donors who will participate at the lower ranges of your scale of giving model. The variety and frequency of your campaign communications become even more important as you continue to build and maintain momentum for your effort.

Plan the Public Campaign Phase Early

Too many inexperienced nonprofits will launch a capital campaign without thoroughly planning what strategies will occur during the public phase. And if those plans haven't been outlined in detail, those in charge can "hit a brick wall," falling far short of the goal and not knowing how the balance of funds will be raised.

Assuming that 50 percent or more of the goal will be raised during the quiet (pre-announcement) phase, break down how the remaining funds will be raised once the campaign becomes public. Assigning those needed dollars to specific strategies will help determine if your plans are adequate.

The example shown here helps to illustrate key actions to be taken during the public phase of a campaign. A true public phase action plan should reveal even more detail.

For a Better Tomorrow Campaign

Campaign goal..$5 million
Raised to date (Quiet Phase)......................................$3 million
Balance to be raised (Public Phase)............................$2 million

Public Phase Action Plan	Goal
Personal calls.......100 individuals/businesses............$1,500,000 ($5,000-$99,999 prospects)	
Telesolicitation......$1,000-$4,999 prospects...............$150,000 (Personal calls if local)	
Direct mail appeal.....remaining constituency..............$100,000	
Special events (2)..........gala, golf classic........................$250,000	
	$2,000,000

Create a Campaign Announcement Checklist

Before you get to that magic moment of publicly announcing your capital campaign — when you have achieved 50 percent or more of your overall goal — create a checklist of strategies to initiate as that time draws near.

Here are some examples of campaign announcement activities to review as you develop your own checklist:

❑ Prepare announcement news releases and press packets for the media.
❑ Assemble a list of media to be invited.
❑ Formulate strategies for securing more far-reaching media attention of the announcement (e.g., matching challenge, largest gift in community's history, impact of the campaign's completion on the state/region, etc.).
❑ Assemble a list of constituency members and dignitaries to be invited to the announcement ceremonies.

❑ Decide who will be a part of the announcement program.
❑ Determine how to announce the campaign to distant friends who can't attend.
❑ Decide how to involve the board and lead donors in the announcement.
❑ Have all campaign materials prepared.
❑ Determine how to best showcase the site/project to be impacted by the campaign (e.g., groundbreaking ceremony, a tour of the site, etc.).
❑ Assist CEO/others in preparation of a compelling campaign announcement.
❑ Develop strategies to maintain the public momentum of the campaign after its announcement.

CAMPAIGN

Publicly Announcing Your Campaign... With Enthusiasm

Campaign Kick-off Event Offers Chance to Highlight Major Gift

Officials at the Saint Louis Zoo (St. Louis, MO) kicked off the public phase of its $120 million, seven-year Living Promise Campaign with the announcement of the largest single charitable gift in the history of the zoo: a $5 million, multi-year gift from long-time corporate supporter Emerson (St. Louis, MO).

"This was the perfect opportunity to announce the largest gift we had received during the quiet phase of the campaign," says Cynthia Holter, the zoo's vice president of external relations. "Emerson has been a long-standing supporter of the Saint Louis Zoo and a high-profile member of the corporate community, so we were thrilled to be able to announce their generous gift in this very public way."

Officials announced the gift at a campaign kickoff at the World's Fair Pavilion in Forest Park, MO, that featured entertainment from a Grammy-nominated composer performing with an orchestra and a short campaign video featuring images of the proposed new animal exhibits and expansion of the elephant habitat. Music drove the video's animation, Holter says. "For each note of the music, the animation responded, as if alive and interacting with the music. Animated animals appeared and magically transformed from color and music into mystical creatures."

Source: Cynthia Holter, Vice President of External Relations, Saint Louis Zoo, St. Louis, MO. E-mail: powell@stlzoo.org

---

Quarter-century Relationship Leads to $5 Million Gift

Cynthia Holter, vice president of external relations, Saint Louis Zoo (St. Louis, MO), shares how a $5 million gift from Emerson (St. Louis, MO) came into being:

"Emerson's relationship with the Saint Louis Zoo goes back over 25 years. Many of their executives have served on our governing boards, and they were a generous supporter to the zoo's last capital campaign.... So it was natural to involve them in our largest fundraising campaign to date. Following a meeting with Emerson executives, we sent them a written proposal with several high-profile projects they might consider funding. They chose the Zooline Railroad. This is a perfect fit for them, since they manufacture a variety of engines and engine parts. We also knew that it would inspire other donors."

Make the Most of Your Capital Campaign Announcement

So far, each step of your capital campaign has unfolded as planned: A long-term strategic plan was developed and from that, a compelling case statement written and shared with major gift prospects and board members.

A capital campaign plan was then developed and endorsed by your board. A steering committee was assembled and its members have quietly been securing lead gifts. According to schedule, you have now secured 50 percent of your campaign goal from board members and a handful of others (as few as 10 percent of your constituency), and you're about to go public with an official announcement of your campaign.

The public announcement of a capital campaign is an important phase of the overall process. It's at this point that you are counting on the remaining 90 percent of your constituency to respond generously with multiyear commitments.

Here are some strategies to help you publicly announce your campaign and get the biggest bang for your buck:

- **Schedule a well-thought-out press conference.** Have board members, your steering committee and major gift participants (to date) on hand for your CEO's public announcement of the campaign. Unveil plans to the media for the use of the funds. Show a scale of giving for the campaign that illustrates as much as 50 percent of the goal has already been met. Distribute campaign press packets. If it can be accomplished, announce a challenge gift that has been established in which all future commitments will be matched dollar for dollar.

- **Personalize the announcement to those you plan to approach.** Send an invitation to area prospects. Minimally, send a personalized letter announcing and explaining the campaign to those you plan to approach. (Do not, however, ask for any kind of commitment at this time.)

- **Periodically announce major gifts that were committed during the quiet phase of the campaign.** To help maintain the campaign's momentum following the announcement, schedule weekly or monthly announcements of major gifts and feature stories on how they will be earmarked for the campaign. Focus on how their gifts will benefit those served by your organization.

- **Inform prospects outside of your immediate area.** If you are counting on the help of individuals, businesses or foundations from outside of your immediate geographic area, take steps to include them in the public announcement of your campaign. Send a video of the campaign announcement. Schedule area receptions to restage the announcement for those in each location.

- **Enlist solicitor volunteers who have or will make exemplary gifts during this most visible period.** Now that you have approached the most major gift prospects during the pre-announcement phase, enlist those prospects on the next level of financial capability as volunteers in your effort. Approach them individually for their commitments and willingness to become involved as volunteers. They will tend to contribute more sacrificially if they become involved in and own your campaign and, likewise, will be better volunteer solicitors if they have made exemplary commitments themselves.

Publicly Announcing Your Campaign... With Enthusiasm

Announce a New Gift as You Go Public With Capital Campaign

In fundraising, as in comedy, timing is everything.

Timing is especially important when announcing a major campaign — you want donors to hear about your campaign at a time when a) they are excited to give, and b) they feel their donation will make the greatest impact.

For these reasons, the timing was perfect for officals at the Saint Louis Zoo, who recently announced the public phase of their $120 million campaign under the best of circumstances. Not only were they able to announce making well over half of their goal during the private phase of their campaign, they also announced a handful of record-breaking major gifts, all on the 100th anniversary of the zoo's opening in 1910.

"We don't have elaborate events all the time," explains Cynthia Holter, director of external relations, at the zoo, referring to the large centennial gala her team put together, "It all sort of culminated." Holter explains that her team launched the $120 million campaign's quiet phase in 2007, and had hoped to be ready to announce it by the centennial celebration. Then, when the $5 million gift came in, the donor requested the announcement be saved for the celebration as well.

"We wanted a chance to honor the guests in a really special way," she says, "not just the $5 million gift, but also a $1 million corporate gift, and a $3 million bequest, as well as the many donors that came out of the woodwork to support the zoo in time for the event. It was huge for us."

The event itself was a major production complete with Grammy award-winning music and fireworks. Holter made sure that donors at all levels were invited.

"For these events," she says, "we've found the more the merrier. Even those who haven't given large gifts are worthy of

---

Minicampaigns: Mobilize Donations Around Event Deadlines

Planning a major non-fundraising event? You can still use the opportunity to encourage immediate giving.

Cynthia Holter, director of external relations at the Saint Louis Zoo (St. Louis, MO), shares how her organization's centennial anniversary celebration allowed her to mobilize donors who had been waiting to give:

"We used the event as a sort of deadline, letting people know that we would be including donor names in the program for this major event, and if they wanted to be recognized at that time, they could give before June 3."

The effort inspired 25 donors to give between the announcement and deadline, including four major bequests valued at $7.5 million, $1.3 million, $725,000 and $389,000.

---

being recognized. And as we talk to people about bequests, we let them know they can turn some of those bequests into cash gifts for more recognition opportunities. We want people to think, I have the zoo in my estate plan, I should tell them."

The event was a success. Holter received 30 e-mails and numerous calls from donors the next morning, thanking her for a lovely time and a great evening; she even heard from several new donors. "The event and the announcement got people talking," Holter says. "It was very much worth it."

Source: Cynthia Holter, Director of External Relations, Saint Louis Zoo, St. Louis, MO. E-mail: holter@stlzoo.org

Use a Challenge to Launch Your Major Capital Campaign

When you receive a life-changing gift, do all you can to maximize its impact.

When the United Way of Central Carolinas (Charlotte, NC) received an unsolicited $1 million matching challenge grant from the Leon Levine Foundation in support of its Community Care Fund Campaign just before the campaign kickoff, officials used the challenge grant to garner new support for the campaign by matching every dollar raised above the 2008 Community Care Fund amount.

"The grant added excitement, momentum and focus for our fundraising efforts this year," says Dani Stone, the United Way chapter's vice president of marketing. "Receiving this generous grant from the highly respected Leon Levine Foundation certainly helped us kick off our campaign in a very positive way. The grant provides a doubling effect for donors and provides an opportunity to set a new kind of goal — one that is focused on the Community Care Fund (undesignated dollars) from the outset, and not simply on the number of total dollars raised."

Focusing on the Community Care Fund, she says, helps pro-

vide a platform for continuity of the organization's core mission and helps build awareness and media coverage of the importance of supporting their local member agencies. One hundred percent of the dollars raised over last year's goal will go directly to the member agencies they serve.

Another reason for making the challenge grant part of the campaign kick-off, Stone says, was to begin soliciting companies that choose to participate in advance of pacesetter companies or at the very start of the United Way's official campaign season.

"We did not want to delay the announcement of the grant and miss opportunities with those donors and those workplace campaigns," she says. "The earlier we were able to share the announcement, the earlier we were able to focus on the Community Care Fund and ask donors to consider supporting it."

Source: Dani Stone, Vice President of Marketing, United Way of Central Carolinas, Charlotte, NC.
E-mail: dstone@uwcentralcarolinas.org

CAMPAIGN

Publicly Announcing Your Campaign... With Enthusiasm

Online Campaign Launch Reaches Broad Audience

Live video, online chat rooms, pictures, games and prizes were all part of a first-of-its-kind online event announcing the launch of the Bold. Brilliant. Binghamton Campaign for Binghamton University, State University of New York (Binghamton, NY).

"We were looking for something different for our campaign launch," says Rebecca Benner, campaign director, "something that would make a big splash and would reach a broad audience, but would be cost-effective."

On April 22, 2010, organizers unveiled the campaign's public phase by launching a website made specifically for the event.

"We contracted with an event consultant who had done many extravagant launches and inaugurations, but was exploring ways to utilize technology to create an event experience in a virtual world," says Benner.

Once logged on viewers could watch a live, streamed announcement of the campaign goal; clever videos featuring dozens of university faculty, staff, students and donors; photos of the campus, Binghamton-themed games; and a video contest where anyone could submit their 60-second Bold and Brilliant video for a $1,000 prize.

"The event had to be very interactive to hold the attention of the attendees. We included very little text and a lot of video content, games and the opportunity to communicate with peers and favorite professors," says Benner.

A welcome video provided an introduction to the various components available while a Twitter feed and chat rooms hosted by Binghamton faculty, students and alumni kept many entertained. "The most popular feature of the event was the "party rooms" or chat rooms which focused on either a featured faculty members or affinity groups. The various affinity groups certainly helped spread the word to enhance participation at the event," says Benner.

The campaign's goal is $95 million, with $42 million supporting student excellence, $45 million for faculty and academic programs and $8 million to fund current operations. At the launch event, Benner says, campaign officials announced they had already raised $82.9 million during the quiet phase of the campaign, which began in 2005. "That left us with just over $12 million to raise during the public phase. The event itself was not a fundraiser, but we certainly had a 'Make a Gift' link on the event website which resulted in a dozen or so gifts during the event," Benner says.

The campaign, which runs through June 2012, has raised some $87 million to date.

While Benner calls the online campaign launch a success, she cites several factors she would change next time: "It would have been great to have had more chat rooms available based on interests/affinities. We also wish we would have scripted the live broadcast a bit more. It was a little too hard to follow for those viewing it remotely."

Source: Rebecca Benner, Campaign Director, Binghamton University, State University of New York, Binghamton, NY.
E-mail: rbenner@binghamton.edu

Campaign Ask Rule of Thumb

■ In a capital campaign, it is generally acceptable to ask a regular donor to your organization for a 30 percent increase over his/her previous cumulative gift totals.

Successful Capital Campaigns: From Start to Finish — 3rd Edition

CAMPAIGN

Communications Crucial to Maintaining Momentum

The role of campaign communications is critically important during the public phase of your fundraising effort. Those communications methods should be varied and ongoing: features in printed publications, updates during public appearances, one-on-one meetings, area news coverage, speaking engagements with civic groups and at area gatherings, website updates and more. Likewise, the topics related to your capital campaign should be varied: construction updates, how partiuclar investments will impact those served by your organization, stories about donors and their commitment to your cause, the economic impact of the campaign, etc..

Creatively Share Campaign Progress Updates

Mailings, e-mails or websites don't typically prompt major donors to write checks — people do, says Diane Benninghoff, assistant vice president for advancement, Colorado College (Colorado Springs, CO), which is in the middle of a $300 million capital campaign. "People make major commitments when someone sits down with them one-on-one, matching their passion with the vision of the institution."

But once donors make a major gift in your major campaign, how can you keep them informed on the campaign's progress?

Colorado College officials chose a method that meshes with the institution's connection to the great outdoors: a hiking-themed celebration. "We had a big party on campus when we reached the midway point raising $145 million. We had a portable climbing wall, an oxygen bar and people were even asked to wear hiking boots," says Benninghoff.

To update the campaign's progress, they used the analogy of a trail map. "We told people we were at the timberline now, and in order to reach the summit, it would be a steep climb, but can be done," she says. College officials posted the map/progress chart on its website and continue to update it as the campaign progresses.

"We don't expect people to become an investor because they looked at the website or saw the updates," she says. "It's more about keeping people informed and seeing how their gift might fit into the grand plan."

They also provide periodic video messages from the school's president, updating progress as well as providing a ba-

sic knowledge and understanding of the school's plan to achieve its vision. "The website mimics the kind of presentation we give to potential major gifts donors. But we don't expect people to donate just from what they see on the website. Major gifts result when a relationship has been established," says Benninghoff.

When making a major gift announcement or other important institutional news, she says they inform the board of trustees first. Next, they share it with campus, members of the President's Circle and other leaders. The general population of donors is informed by an alumni magazine, the website and a monthly electronic newsletter. "If there is really big news, we will issue a special edition of the electronic newsletter to announce it."

School officials also periodically hold events to thank the people who are helping achieve the campaign's vision, says Benninghoff.

She says that while they do not send a campaign newsletter to update progress, they give updates in the alumni magazine, mailings and e-mails. Annual giving solicitations are tied to the campaign's priorities because everyone is a part of the effort. Benninghoff says, "Every time there is a mailing or e-mail, we notice a spike in annual giving."

Source: Diane Benninghoff, Assistant Vice President for Advancement, Colorado College, Colorado Springs, CO.
E-mail: DBenninghoff@ColoradoCollege.edu

Items to Include on Your Capital Campaign Website

- ❑ Your organization's strategic plan
- ❑ Campaign objectives/goals/priorities
- ❑ Campaign news (gifts received so far, kickoff events, etc.)
- ❑ Giving opportunities; ways to give
- ❑ Copy of the Donor Bill of Rights
- ❑ Contact information
- ❑ Campaign goal
- ❑ Campaign progress chart
- ❑ Case for support
- ❑ Forms for naming opportunities, etc.
- ❑ Donor profiles

- ❑ President's campaign message
- ❑ Video of campaign kickoff speeches, ground breaking, construction, etc.
- ❑ Campaign co-chairs and volunteers
- ❑ Campaign overview
- ❑ Campaign logo and tagline
- ❑ Campaign press releases, media kit
- ❑ PDFs of campaign publications (brochure, newsletter, etc.)
- ❑ Online donation page
- ❑ Architectural sketches, donor photos, progress charts, etc.
- ❑ Testimonials (donors, constituents, clients, students, staff, etc.)

Communications Crucial to Maintaining Momentum

Aid Campaign Solicitations With Architectural Renderings

The case for architectural renderings is simple, says Anna Loseva, an architectural illustrator with Art and Design Studios (Tanersville, PA): Having visual representation of a project helps raise funds.

"It's one thing to approach donors with a story, it's another to have a story and images," she says. "Architectural visualizations can be the difference between the success or failure of a project's financing request."

Loseva shares expert insight into this vital component of any construction-based capital campaign.

What are the different types of architectural renderings and how do they compare to one another?

"The main division these days is between computer rendering and hand rendering. With computers, the end result is very realistic and photographic. This can be an advantage in some situations, but you need to have designed the space to that level of detail. So if you're still in the early stages of the process, computer rendering is difficult to do.

Also, in many cases the owner or architect does not want to imply a design is finished. They want to give food for the donor's imagination and make an attractive impression, but they also want people to understand that the design is still subject to change, so they choose ink or watercolor. Hand rendering can be very sketchy or very detailed, but either way, it often has a feel of impression or suggestiveness, where digital rendering has a feel of believability."

Are there particular views or depictions that make a bigger emotional impact?

"It depends on the project. If you're building a skyscraper in Manhattan, you want to show the skyline and how the new building will be recognizable in it. For an institution opening a new campus (college, research, medical), you usually want an aerial view that shows landscaping elements and how the project fits the surrounding cityscape or natural landscape. For smaller projects like a single building, you want to show the exterior from fairly close, along with snapshots of interiors like the cafeteria, gym or lobby."

What might the process of collaborating with an architectural illustrator like yourself be like?

"It starts with architectural documents being transferred to us. Once we have studied these, we come up with sketches, discuss them with the owner and get any feedback. Once views are selected, we start developing the drawings, then render them in color, usually watercolor. We then photograph the renderings, tweak them in Photoshop, and deliver the final product in digital format."

At what point in the design process should renderings be developed?

"As soon as the architect has been engaged. The architect will guide the development process by asking key questions like: How many square feet? High-rise or low-rise? Modern or traditional? He will also be the one to find a good illustrator, if he doesn't already have a relationship with one."

What could an organization expect to pay for architectural illustrations?

"It depends on level of detail and complexity. A large museum atrium or shopping mall could include a scene of 50 people, where the lobby of a small nonprofit might only have four or five. But color images will range from $2,000 to $4,000 on average, and black-and-white drawings will be $1,000 to $2,000."

Source: Anna Loseva, Architectural Illustrator, Art and Design Studios, Tanersville, PA. E-mail: Aloseva@yahoo.com

Get the Most From Your Illustrations

Veterans of major capital campaigns know that a few high-quality architectural illustrations can do wonders for a case statement or major gift solicitation. But you might be surprised to learn that renderings can contribute to fundraising efforts in other ways.

Anna Loseva, architectural illustrator with Art and Design Studios (Tanersville, PA) explains how.

"The original of a good hand illustration can be sold or gifted to major donors because it's an art piece in a way that the print-out of a computer illustration is not. You can also print a limited number of digital images on special watercolor paper that ends up looking like a beautiful watercolor painting. These can be numbered, signed by the illustrator, framed, and sold or gifted to donors as limited-edition prints."

Content not available in this edition

Content not available in this edition

Shown above are two examples of architectural renderings provided by Art and Design Studios. The top image is of the Newman University (Wichita, KS) campus expansion and the bottom is the new pool for Overbrook School for the Blind (Philadelphia, PA).

Communications Crucial to Maintaining Momentum

Capital Campaigns, Major Gifts and the Role of Social Media

Social media is one of the hottest trends in nonprofit communications. It is used to reach to numerous stakeholders in a variety of situations. But what role should it have in large capital campaigns, particularly in connection with major donors? Major gifts need real relationships, not virtual ones, says Robert Moore, president and CEO of the Chicago, IL-based marketing firm Lipman Hearne. But he says virtual interactions have many benefits outside direct solicitation that should not be overlooked: They add dimension and constancy to ongoing relationships; they inform and raise awareness; and they create channels for interactive dialogue, to name just a few.

Here Moore addresses a variety of topics related to social media and its integration with capital campaigns and major gift fundraising.

On the most effective role for social media in a capital campaign —
"While inappropriate to the actual solicitation of gifts, social media can be very helpful in the introduction, informing and engaging stages of the moves-management process. It can create a buzz about the organization that pays dividends when you get into the personal conversations of cultivation work. People feel like you are an active and relevant organization because they've seen you in the social media landscape, and that can be very reinforcing for a major gift officer making a pitch. Handled right, social media can really increase engagement and dialogue in a campaign."

On how social media can augment gift officers' more traditional activities —
"If you're a major gift officer with a portfolio of 50 or 70 prospects, social media can help you stay in touch more than you would otherwise. It can help you stay at the forefront of their minds. You can also use prospects' social media actions as the seeds for more personal conversations: 'I saw you liked the article we posted on Facebook last week.' Social media can be used to feed information to prospects, monitor their responses, and help elevate your message above the digital noise they receive every day."

On how social media can establish or reinforce a campaign's brand —
"The whole idea of a campaign brand is that this is a special moment of time in which to push an institution forward. Social media can really reinforce the urgency of that message, addressing the campaign's core issues, looking at its impact and extending its narrative through different channels. It can be used to continually reinforce the message that you're not just raising $1 billion, you're raising $1 billion to do something of significance."

On what an effective social media approach targeting major donors might look like —
"Say you're an environmental organization dedicated to protecting natural resources. You could invite your constituents to submit a personal 'ocean story' via YouTube video, something like a clip of them standing waist-deep in the ocean of their choice and talking about why it matters to them. Now, your major donors are probably not going to be the ones standing in the water. But they are going to be looking at dozens of people who are, and that kind of engaged, authentic content is very powerful."

On the biggest misconceptions nonprofits have about using social media in major capital campaigns —
"I frequently see a lack of understating about how much effort a social media presence takes. You can't just have a website and post press releases on it. The essence of social media is dialogue and responsiveness, not just pushing information at people. And that back-and-forth takes commitment and effort."

On what to avoid when using social media with major campaign donors —
"I wouldn't push it too hard. You can introduce it to major donors, but if they're not interested, that's fine. Social media is voluntary, and you want to make sure your primary objective is creating productive sit-down conversations. That's where the business really takes place, and social media should always be used as a means to get there."

Source: Robert Moore, President and CEO, Lipman Hearne, Chicago, IL. E-mail: Rmoore@lipmanhearne.com

Foundation Challenge Gifts Help Carry Momentum

Once you have at least 50 percent of your campaign goal in hand and you have announced the public phase of your campaign, consider going after challenge grants from foundations (e.g., Kresge Foundation) to help carry you through to the end.

A challenge grant from a foundation has threefold benefits:

1. Putting your foundation proposal in the form of a challenge may be what it takes to secure the foundation grant.

2. Doing so can help motivate new pledges throughout your campaign's public phase.

3. In addition to new pledges, you may be able to make return visits to those who made lead gifts, inviting them to up their pledges in response to the challenge grant.

CAMPAIGN

Communications Crucial to Maintaining Momentum

How to Get Permission to Publicize Major Gifts

We in the fundraising industry recognize the value of publicizing major gifts. News of a major gift can raise your organization's status as a viable philanthropic recipient, help advertise your campaign and encourage a healthy sense of competition among potential donors.

But what if a major donor exhibits reluctance to have his/her gift publicized?

According to many major gifts experts, nonprofits have four approaches to consider for encouraging donors to allow their gifts to be publicized. Your challenge is to glean which of these approaches will best appeal to your donor, remembering, above all, to let the donor be your guide.

The four approaches are to:

1. **Share examples of past gift giving.** Gently begin this conversation with your donor by sharing examples of other donations, and the stories of the donors who made them. This may help to put the idea of publicity into a greater context for the donor.

2. **Express publicity in terms of audience and goals, rather than medium.** Often, shy donors hesitate to announce gifts, because they aren't interested in the attention publicity may garner. Help your donor see the benefits of publicity in terms of the message it sends, rather than the accolades it may bring. You can even let the donor choose where and to whom he/she wants the gift to be announced.

3. **Share and brainstorm new gift announcements.** Your donor may have a fixed idea as to what a gift announcement looks like. As discussed in No. 2, gift announcements should be tailored to the audience and goal for which the gift was given. Your donor may be inspired by an artful announcement, or an announcement that challenges others to match the gift, in a way that he/she did not realize was possible.

4. **Encourage anonymous giving.**
   Ultimately, if a donor wishes to remain anonymous, it is in your best interest to respect and even encourage that preference. Anonymous donors have a certain freedom with giving, and when they recognize that your organization is willing to work with them in that desire, they may be more likely to give in the future, and in greater amounts.

Allow Donors to Share in Accomplishments

Whether you are completing a successful capital campaign or simply working at landing more major gifts, it's important for donors to share in your organization's accomplishments. After all, it's their major investments that make possible some of your organization's most impressive achievements.

Be sure your donors are aware of and take ownership in each of your organization's accomplishments. If it's not possible to see each of your donors face to face, craft a personalized letter signed by your CEO or board chair that delineates major accomplishments during the past year or so. Send it to those who generously gave of their resources and give them the credit they deserve for those accomplishments.

Dear Jack and Ellen:

This has been a remarkable year for Emerson Boys and Girls Home. In fact, thanks to friends such as you, it's been a transformational year. Because of your generosity, our agency has established a regional reputation that is attracting immeasurable positive attention.

Allow me to give a partial rundown of what's been happening at Emerson thanks to you and others:

✓ Completion of a $3.5 million expansion allowing us to serve an ever-growing population of young people who desperately need our services.

✓ The addition of $750,000 to Emerson's endowment which will allow us to not only maintain our past level of services but enhance them even more.

✓ The most positive certification review Emerson has ever received in its 52-year history.

✓ A significantly increased success rate of improved academic standing among former clients.

✓ An annual membership that has grown by 31 percent in the past 24 months.

✓ The addition of more talented, highly skilled personnel.

I could go on, but you get the picture. And don't for one minute think that you didn't play a role in all of this. You did! And we value your partnership to very much.

Dr. Erik Erikson said, "Children love and want to be loved and they very much prefer the joy of accomplishment to the triumph of hateful failure." Those of us who make up the Emerson family — you among them — also prefer the joy of accomplishment. Thank you for continuing to make that joy possible.

Sincerely,

Communications Crucial to Maintaining Momentum

PhotoBooth Project Enhances Capital Campaign, Much More

The PhotoBooth project began as a simple way to reinforce the Thanks to Berkeley ... theme of the University of California, Berkeley's $3 billion capital campaign. But it came to be used in a dizzying array of contexts, and ended up winning the CASE grand gold award for institution-wide branding.

"It's basically a collection of beautiful portraits of students, alumni and faculty accompanied by a 10-words-or-less message of thanks to Berkeley in their own handwriting," says Mary Keegan, executive director of marketing and communications. "The idea was to create more visibility for the campaign on campus and among the public."

Keegan explains that the university partnered with a San Francisco-area photographer to stage in-person PhotoBooth events, both on campus and at major donor events around the country. The events provided an opportunity to capture the photos and quotes, but also furthered the campaign itself, she says. "People understand it better from having had that real, physical experience of going into the booth and connecting in this way."

Photos from the first several installations were used in 74-foot, double-sided billboards that were unveiled as part of the capital campaign's grand kickoff. Several thousand more pictures (currently over 3,000) have been taken since that time. These can be viewed, searched and downloaded in a scrolling montage-display on the campaign's website.

Keegan says the project has provided a rich source of content and photography for the campaign. She notes that the photos have been used in direct mail pieces, philanthropy reports, gift acknowledgement cards, annual parents' reports and alumni magazines. They have been made into wallpaper positioned behind presentations, and crafted into large, internally-lit light boxes. And development offices have also had success inviting booth participants to personally read their messages to supporters and event attendees.

The PhotoBooth project accomplished its primary objective of creating a stronger culture of giving at Berkeley. But Keegan says it did more than that. "The word most commonly mentioned in the quotes was 'diversity,' and the photos show that incredible diversity in black-and-white. They make it plain for everybody to see why Berkeley is such an amazing place."

Source: Mary Keegan, Executive Director, Marketing and Communications, University of California, Berkeley, Berkeley, CA. E-mail: mkeegan@berkeley.edu

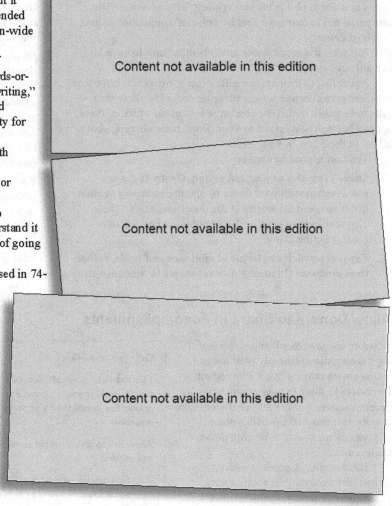

The images and quotes collected in the University of California, Berkeley's PhotoBooth project have been used in a wide variety of ways.

CAMPAIGN

Communications Crucial to Maintaining Momentum

Challenge Takes Advantage of Capital Campaign Momentum

Riding the momentum of a recent capital campaign, a giving challenge made to parents of students attending Blair Academy (Blairstown, NJ) broke giving records.

"We had just come off a campaign and wanted to keep the momentum going," says Sue Habermann, director of capital giving and past director of parent relations, of the challenge. "Many times schools start challenges later in the year if they aren't meeting goals, but we decided to start ours at the beginning of the school year to keep that campaign energy going and invigorate our volunteers."

An anonymous group of parents established a $200,000 challenge grant for the 2009-10 school years, she says. "In the past, we've had tremendous success from our parents who see the direct results of their children's education." This challenge, she notes, gave parents reason to support the students, along with incentive to boost annual fund participation to a new level.

The challenge matched new gifts dollar for dollar up to $2,000, generated an additional $500 for increased gifts of any size, and included a $10,000 gift added to any first-time gift of $10,000 or more.

School officials informed parents of the challenge through the school's fall appeal, parent newsletter, website and a special meeting on Parents' Weekend. Habermann says the most successful method for sharing the challenge information was parents calling other parents.

Initiated in October 2009, the challenge ran through June 2010, which was six months longer than originally planned, Habermann says, noting, "The challenge was going so well, so the school approached a donor and asked if (he/she) would be willing to extend it."

She says results exceeded Blair officials' expectations, with the challenge raising $337,474 in matching funds. Sixty-one percent of current parents increased their gift from the prior year and 78 percent of new parents made a gift. Also, 20 parents each gave a first-time gift of $10,000.

The challenge also helped push Blair Fund parent giving past the $1 million mark for the first time, to a record $1,110,408 with 81 percent participation.

Source: Sue Habermann, Director of Capital Giving, Blair Academy, Blairstown, NJ. E-mail: habers@blair.edu

Periodic 'Scale of Giving' Report Helps Visualize Progress

Capital campaigns often begin with a scale-of-giving chart that projects what gifts will be required in various gift ranges in order to achieve the campaign goal. The chart can be custom designed to fit the anticipated gifts that a charity will receive based on the results of a feasibility study.

As a capital campaign gets under way and progresses, the scale-of-giving chart can also serve as the basis for ongoing reports, comparing anticipated giving with actual gifts received. This helps development personnel (and others involved in the campaign) understand where the campaign is on track and where it might be missing the mark.

Make ongoing use of a scale-of-giving progress report such as the one shown here. You will find it to be a useful monitoring tool.

Scale-of-Giving Progress Report

Campaign Goal: $5 million
Gifts/Pledges As Of _____

No. of Gifts Needed	Gift Range	Total	Actual To Date	Needed
4	$ 500,000	$ 2 million	1/$500,000	$1.5 million
4	$ 250,000	$ 1 million	2/$250,000	$ 500,000
10	$ 100,000	$ 1 million 1/$150,000	3/$100,000	$ 550,000
10	$ 50,000	$ 500,000	3/$50,000	$ 350,000
12	$ 25,000	$ 300,000 1/$30,000	4/$25,000	$ 170,000
20 60	Less Than $25,000	$ 200,000 $ 5 million	7/$10,000 23/$1,800,000	$ 130,000 $3,200,000

Successful Capital Campaigns: From Start to Finish, Third Edition.
Edited by Scott C. Stevenson.
© 2012 Stevenson, Inc. Published 2012 by Stevenson, Inc.

Successful Capital Campaigns: From Start to Finish — 3rd Edition

POST-CAMPAIGN

Bringing the Campaign to a Successful Close

The way you draw a capital campaign to a close is frankly as important as the way in which it gets underway. It's important to keep the public involved as fully as possible as your effort reaches and perhaps surpasses its goal. That includes collective and individual recognition of donors and volunteers, open houses, tours, topping-off ceremonies, periodic updates on the impact of the campaign and more. Enthusiasm and momentum should carry through to post-campaign activities — even if staff never want to hear the word campaign again! Your campaign conclusion will serve as the thread to a future campaign, whenever that takes place.

Ideas for Maintaining Capital Campaign Momentum

You're two, three, even five years into a capital campaign, and everyone is starting to feel the grind. Even if your campaign is on track to make its goal, re-establishing a vibrant sense of momentum can be the difference between stumbling across the finish line and surging to a triumphant and memorable victory.

Below are a few ideas, drawn from major ongoing capital campaigns, for reviving flagging momentum.

- **Highlight progress already made.** Five years into a seven-year, $5 billion campaign, Columbia University (New York, NY) summarizes its progress by the numbers with easy-to-grasp infographics in areas like annual giving, professorships and new facilities.

- **Elevate your target.** Sometimes organizations find themselves in the enviable position of slowing down because a campaign is on pace to meet its goal well ahead of schedule. In such cases, raising the overall campaign

target is a good way to maintain focus and momentum. This is what Columbia University did by extending The Columbia Campaign by two years and $1 billion.

- **Remind stakeholders why they care.** The $3 billion campaign for the University of California, Berkeley (Berkeley, CA) encourages students, faculty and alumni to express their gratitude to the university through its PhotoBooth Project — a collection of thousands of pictures presented in a continuously scrolling montage, each of which can be clicked to display a larger image and a short handwritten message of thanks from the individual.

- **Thank supporters — then thank them again.** This minute-long video, which was included in the 2011 report of the campaign for the University of Oxford (Oxford, UK), features dozens of clips of students, staff and faculty members, but uses only two spoken words: "Thank you."

Reinvigorate the Later Stages Of a Long Campaign

Capital and endowment campaigns are sometimes described as extraordinary efforts to raise an extraordinary amount of funds for extraordinary needs — a definition that is characterized by a clear and compelling sense of urgency. But in campaigns that last five, seven, sometimes ten years, maintaining that sense of urgency (and instilling it in prospects) can be challenging. Shorter campaigns are one answer, but if you are currently in the middle of a long effort, don't be afraid to shake things up with mid-stream changes. Whether this is as simple as producing a new video or mailer, or as extensive as undertaking a full-blown rebranding effort, anything done to restore that sense of forward momentum will help ignite fading enthusiasm.

Five Ways to Jumpstart Stalled Campaigns

It's not uncommon for a campaign to get bogged down in the final months. That's when it becomes necessary for you to re-energize everyone involved and determine what additional steps are needed.

1. **Meet with your volunteer fundraisers.** Are they making calls? If not, why? If they're uncomfortable calling on prospects, role play. If they are hitting resistance, share ideas for turning "no" or "maybe" into "yes."

2. **Meet with your CEO.** Is he/she making calls? Still invested in the campaign? If not, redirect his/her efforts. Without the CEO's support, the campaign will fail.

3. **Review your donor list to see who might give more.** It's possible that some current donors will want to up their pledges, especially if some time has gone by since their original pledges were made.

4. **Create a sense of urgency.** Develop a campaign strategy that sets a deadline for receiving X number of dollars; get a donor to make a deadline-specific challenge grant.

5. **Use current gifts to encourage new gifts.** Build new enthusiasm by getting your current major donors involved in publicizing their gifts and their reasons for giving.

POST-CAMPAIGN

Bringing the Campaign to a Successful Close

Post-campaign Priorities

Your work doesn't end when your campaign does. Here are six key post-campaign priorities:

1. **Send reminders each month a payment is due.** Make them personal, positive updates that state total gift, amount paid to date and balance.

2. **Keep publishing your campaign newsletter** to keep all donors informed on project progress and tell why continued support is crucial.

3. **Track donors of one-time cash gifts.** Contact them on their gift anniversary to see if they would consider supporting a specific part of the project or general operating needs.

4. **Publish fundraising and pledge redemption results.** Let donors know how close you are to collecting all needed funds.

5. **Hold periodic building events.** Have ground blessings, ground breakings and onsite celebrations to keep enthusiasm high and emphasize original reasons for the campaign and how close you are to the goal as pledges are paid.

6. **Close outstanding solicitation visits.** Revisit prospects who have not pledged to re-explain the importance of their support. Revisit nonpaying donors with the same leaders who received their initial gift.

No Campaign End-date? No Problem!

Most seasoned fundraisers will say that creating a sense of urgency among donors and prospects is key to a successful campaign. But that doesn't necessarily require a hard-and-fast deadline hanging overhead, as evidenced by the Creating Futures campaign of the University of Colorado.

"The urgency comes from the challenging economy," says Patrick Kramer, vice president of development and campaigns at the University of Colorado Foundation (Boulder, CO). "It comes from the number of years since our last campaign and from the fact that only about 5 percent of higher education is supported by the state of Colorado."

Kramer explains that the $1.5 billion campaign weathered a number of false starts during its initial stages, and organizers felt that leaving it open-ended would help maintain momentum and insulate it from negative effects in a historically uncertain economy.

But the decision was also part of a wider strategy aimed at de-emphasizing the internal mechanics of the campaign and focusing instead on its tangible impact. "We did a milestone announcement about reaching $1 billion, but we really didn't do that much publicity about it. Similarly, we're not going to tout our $1.5 billion dollar goal," says Kramer. "Everybody is doing big campaigns — what does that matter to donors? We want our communications to be about the impact donors' support will have, not just the number of dollars involved."

And donors' response to the campaign's non-traditional approach? "We prepared our gift officers to field questions about the lack of an end date, but it simply hasn't been an issue," he says. "Our major donors truly understand why we're raising money and they're happy to do their part."

He adds that the open-ended structure has even helped the solicitation process in some ways. "Sometimes gift officers drop proposals not because the donors are ready for them, but because they are backed up against a deadline. Not having an end date has taken that pressure off and helped us put more focus on identifying and responding to donors' real needs and passions."

The Creating Futures campaign launched in 2006. It went public in 2011 with $900 million raised, and organizers project a total duration of about seven to eight years.

Source: Patrick Kramer, Vice President of Development, Campaigns, University of Colorado Foundation, Boulder, CO.
E-mail: patrick.kramer@cufund.org

Address Additional Objectives With a Parallel Campaign

If your organization has a variety of strategic objectives to meet, consider launching a secondary initiative designed to run in parallel with your primary campaign. That's what the University of Colorado did by pairing the CU in the Future planned giving initiative with its Creating Futures campaign.

Patrick Kramer, vice president of development and campaigns at the University of Colorado Foundation (Boulder, CO) said the initiative was something of a necessity, as the primary campaign did not count unrealized planned gifts toward its $1.5 billion goal. "This gives us a way to recognize and celebrate those gifts, which are of course vital to the institution. And in a time of economic turbulence, planned gifts carry increased appeal."

The two efforts are promoted concurrently and their titles are reminiscent of each other, but Kramer says the funds are never intermixed, and gift officers have been trained to explain to alumni and supporters how they differ.

And while the CU in the Future campaign might occasionally require a bit of explanation, Kramer says it has had a very positive effect on the primary campaign. "We often found that people wanted to make a major gift but felt they weren't liquid enough. So we started looking at planned gifts with them. But once that conversation began and they started digging around in their finances, they came to feel they could make a current gift after all. The planned giving focus, we found, brought people deeper into the discussion about what they could or couldn't do for the campaign."

Bringing the Campaign to a Successful Close

Gift Acknowledgement Protocols Reduce Confusion, Lessen Mistakes

Scott Fendley, Principal, SF Consulting (Eden Prairie, MN), shares a detailed acknowledgement policy he developed for Wabash College (Crawfordsville, IN):

PROTOCOL FOR CAMPAIGN GIFT ACKNOWLEDGEMENT

The baseline or default response to gifts and/or pledges is:

All gifts to the College will be acknowledged by an official receipt thank you letter within two working days of the arrival of the gift on campus.

Annual donors of $250-999 will receive a letter from the Chair of the ... Foundation at the beginning of the month after the gift is received. ...

Donors of $1,000+ will receive a letter from the Chair of the 1832 Society at the beginning of the month after the gift is received. (Trustees will not receive this letter). Any changes in gift club status will be noted.

Phonathon pledges will be acknowledged in writing immediately after the pledge is made via handwritten note from student caller who took the pledge.

The Director of the Greater Wabash Foundation will acknowledge all pledges (excluding phonathon pledges) of $1-999.... within 48 hours of receipt.

The Dean for Advancement will review all gifts and pledge payments of $1,000 and above and add personal acknowledgements, as appropriate, within 48 hours of receipt of the gift or pledge payment.

The Chairman of the Campaign will acknowledge outright gifts and pledges of $10,000 and above.

Documented bequests, trusts, life insurance gifts, and other planned giving vehicles that have been confirmed (not matured) shall be acknowledged by the Director of Major Gifts within 48 hours of notification for all gifts up to $100,000. The Dean for Advancement shall acknowledge any confirmed planned gift of $100,000 and above. The Dean for Advancement and the Director of Major and Planned Giving will advise the President of the College regarding the donors he should acknowledge.

The President of the College will be provided a list of all donors who have made a gift of $1,000 or more for his personal acknowledgements.

The Dean for Advancement will acknowledge all gifts and pledges from trustees and members of the board of the National Association of Wabash Men....

The Dean for Advancement and Chairman of the Faculty/Staff Campaign will acknowledge any pledge or gift made by a faculty or staff member. ...

The Dean for Advancement will acknowledge any gift from the Independent Colleges of Indiana.

The Senior Advancement Officer and Coordinator of Volunteer Services will acknowledge any gifts from non-alumni or non-parent owned corporations and all foundations, excluding matching gifts from corporations.

When a matching gift is received, a letter to the donor will be generated and signed by the Director of the Greater Wabash Foundation, excluding trustees. Matching gift companies will receive a receipt only.

Any alumni-owned or parent-owned business that makes a gift will be acknowledged as if the individual owner made the gift.

Letters acknowledging the receipt of memorial gifts, without specifying the gift amount, will be sent to the appropriate person in the family by the Dean for Advancement once a month.

When a gift of stock is made, the valuation ... will be included in the receipt thank you letter, which will be signed by the Dean for Advancement.

If volunteers give their expenses to the College as an in-kind gift instead of reimbursement, the Senior Advancement Officer and Coordinator of Volunteer Services will acknowledge the gift with a thank you letter.

Upon receipt of the final pledge payment (excluding phonathon pledges), a letter of acknowledgement from the Dean for Advancement will be generated thanking the donor for the completion of the pledge.

All letters will be changed quarterly, or as needed to refresh the content and reflect on recent news of the College. These letters will be prepared or reviewed by the Director of Campaign Communications.

(The policy also includes sections detailing special recognition of gifts, as well as how to issue pledge reminders.)

Acknowledging major gifts on the fly may cause important details to fall through the cracks, says Scott Fendley, principal, SF Consulting (Eden Prairie, MN).

That's why organizations should put gift acknowledgement policies in writing. Says Fendley, "Written acknowledgment policies prevent confusion, duplication of efforts, and 'I thought someone else did that,' kinds of situations."

Create policies that are as detailed as possible, he says. Specifically, gift acknowledgement forms should:

- Codify individual staff roles for as many common situations as possible.
- Describe in detail (mailings, signatures, time frames) responses to all gift sizes and program(s) supported.
- Clarify what donors will be invited to what events at what level for different gifts.

Granularity is also important in effective policies, Fendley says, enabling database software to be programmed to automate response actions while ensuring a continuity of response as development staff come and go.

Acknowledgement protocols are particularly useful with more esoteric planned giving vehicles such as memorial gifts, says Fendley, noting that heirs and survivors can be easily overlooked or forgotten.

Acknowledgement policies are best developed by advancement staff with input from senior leadership, says Fendley, and should include input from services and operations staff, as these departments are often involved with implementing, automating, and executing policies.

Source: Scott Fendley, Principal, SF Consulting, Eden Prairie, MN. E-mail: scott@sfconsultingnow.com

Content not available in this edition

POST-CAMPAIGN

Bringing the Campaign to a Successful Close

Create a Schedule of Pledge Redemption Reminders

You surpassed your capital campaign goal. Donors have been properly recognized, and now the campaign is finished. Or is it?

Until all of your donors' pledges have been paid in full, the campaign is not fully finished. Help donors with multi-year pledges by creating a pledge redemption schedule that shows all outstanding pledges along with key information (e.g., payment dates, payment amounts). Many software products are available, or you can simply use an Excel spreadsheet to sort information in a variety of ways. The example shown here has sorted pledge information according to payment due dates.

Having a single place to look will simplify your reminder process and help to ensure friendly reminders are sent in a timely manner.

Pledge Redemption Schedule
Building With Our Hands.... Giving With Our Hearts Campaign

Payment Due	Pledge Period	Final Payment	Donor(s)	Pledge Amount	Payment Amount	Paid To Date	Balance
1/1	3 YR	1/1/13	M. Hartwell	$75,000	$25,000	$50,000	$25,000
2/5	3 YR	2/15/13	Acme Corp.	$300,000	$100,000	$200,000	$100,000
3/10	3 YR	3/10/13	S. Smith	$150,000	$50,000	$100,000	$50,000

Monitor Campaign Pledge Payments Carefully

As you conclude a major fundraising effort, regularly produce and review a pledge payment summary, particularly one that incorporates larger commitments. A spreadsheet similar to the example at right offers the option of sorting pledges and payment schedules a number of ways: alphabetically, by pledge amount, payment schedules, etc.

Regularly reviewing a summary such as this allows you to:

1. Anticipate upcoming notifications for donors who wish to be reminded of scheduled payments.

2. Anticipate cash flow to cover campaign related costs.

3. Identify any donor who may be behind in pledge fulfillment.

4. Identify those who should be groomed for upcoming gift opportunities based on their ending pledge payments.

Campaign Pledge Payment Schedule
Pledges of $10,000 or more

As of_____

DONOR	PAYMENT PLEDGE	PAID SCHEDULE	TO DATE	BALANCE
Altman, John	$50,000	Yearly; 5 yrs; 6/1	$10,000	$40,000
Aston Pharmacy	$30,000	Yearly; 3 yrs; 5/1	$10,000	$20,000
Belner, Debra	$100,000	Yearly; 5 yrs; 9/1	$20,000	$80,000
Bosley, M&L	$250,000	Yearly; 3 yrs; 9/1	$83,334	$166,666
Cameron, L&R	$1 million	Yearly; 3 yrs; 8/1	$350,000	$650,000
Dennis Supply	$500,000	Yearly; 2 yrs; 5/1	$250,000	$250,000
Kipper, Inc.	$75,000	Yearly; 3 yrs; 6/1	$25,000	$50,000
Monson, Albert	$100,000	Yearly; 5 yrs; 9/1	$20,000	$80,000
Straeder, T&E	$30,000	Quarterly; 3 yrs; 5/1	$10,000	$20,000
Wolleson Electric	$50,000	Yearly; 5 yrs; 8/1	$10,000	$40,000
Total	$2,185,000		$788,334	$1,396,666

Bringing the Campaign to a Successful Close

Hard Work, Creativity Combine to Meet Challenge Grant Requirements

Hospice of Southern Illinois, Inc. (Belleville, IL) had raised $5.5 million two-and-a-half years into its $7 million capital campaign to build the first licensed hospice home in Southern Illinois. But when the economy took a downturn, campaign organizers needed to find ways to re-energize campaign supporters and reach their campaign goal.

So Development Manager Susan Reilmann contacted the Kresge Foundation (Troy, MI) to be considered for a Kresge Challenge Grant. The Kresge Foundation selected Hospice of Southern Illinois as the recipient of a $400,000 challenge grant to be awarded if the hospice could complete its $7 million campaign by Dec. 1, 2009.

Reilmann says the hospice's capital campaign consultant, Dee Vandeventer of ME&V Fundraising Advisors (Cedar Falls, IA), was instrumental in their efforts to meet the Kresge Challenge. "Dee became affectionately known as my 'barking dog' and, when necessary, nipped at my heels to move me forward, particularly in the discouragingly low periods of production," she says.

Together Reilmann and Vandeventer devised several strategies for meeting the Kresge Challenge, including:

✓ Updating and creating more enticing naming opportunities, e.g., "Every time a patient's family opens the door to this armoire, your heart will open with joy knowing you have helped create a comfortable environment in a difficult time in their life."

✓ Ramping up their roster of scheduled speaking engagements at which they showed a mission-driven, needs-based video created by ME&V Consultants.

✓ Taking advantage of local bank presidents' contacts by inviting them to lunch and sharing insider campaign information that they could then share with constituents.

✓ Leveraging other challenge grants by asking the community to "help make sure these challenge dollars aren't lost" or leting them know "you can make all the difference in helping us earn these challenge dollars." They used public challenge donors to create friendly rivalries with persons they knew had a relationship with the challenge donor.

✓ Asking board members to make thank-you calls to $1,000-plus donors. "Not only did this effort have a powerful impact on many of the donors, it ultimately sealed a few lifelong gifts via planned giving options," she says. "The most frequent comments from donors were 'Seriously — you're not calling to ask for additional money?' and 'Wow, I've never had a board member call — often a staff person, which is great, but a board member? Thank you for your acknowledgement.'"

✓ Launching a church campaign. Hospice officials asked local churches to make the hospice a recipient of discretionary funds they set aside for special community projects. They also solicited individual church members through meetings with church sub-groups, church bulletins, flyers, and by adding a donation envelope at a worship service where hospice officials were invited to speak. "After hearing about the support offered by their church, many individuals and families contacted us to make personal pledges and donations because they felt if their church endorsed our hospice home, it was worthy of their support," says Reilmann.

One week before the Kresge Challenge deadline, Reilmann used this final strategy to raise the remaining $35,000 needed to fulfill challenge stipulations: She made a personal call to a firm that her campaign team felt could have given more. "I issued them a personal challenge to help us raise the remaining $35,000 in the next week and in return they would receive a big media splash that said congratulations to their company for helping us make the final goal. With the backing of the principals in the firm, they ended up raising nearly $50,000 in that final week. Their strategy was to give each donor a day off during the holidays for each donation or pledge of $1,000 or more."

Reilmann shares a final piece of advice: "Don't be afraid to find and use that vulnerable spot in a company's public image by giving them a way to shine it. Always find a way to make individual donors feel good about your organization and how they can help."

Source: Susan Reilmann, Development Manager, Hospice of Southern Illinois, Inc., Belleville, IL. E-mail: sreilmann@hospice.org

Content not available in this edition

Bringing the Campaign to a Successful Close

Include Donors in Post-campaign Success

Just because your capital campaign has successfully concluded doesn't mean the party's over. It's important to share your campaign's success with donors. After all, their generosity made it a success.

Involve donors in your post-campaign period in the following ways:

- Convey appreciation in a personal way through: personal letters from your organization's CEO, campaign chair and others.

- Follow through on naming gifts with appropriate plaques. Check with donors to be sure names are spelled and listed correctly before authorizing the engraving.

- Invite donors to celebrate in the completion of renovated or newly constructed capital projects to which they contributed. Consider a larger, all-inclusive celebration as well as more individualized gatherings.

- For donors who establish named endowment funds, revisit the details of the fund: how annual interest will be used, the agreed-to name and fund description and such.

Decide on Donor Recognition Prior to Capital Campaign

When someone makes a significant gift, how do you recognize and celebrate that donor's generosity?

One option worth considering is purchasing naming plaques for buildings, rooms, equipment or other items purchased with donors' major gifts.

Ideally, determine exact methods of donor recognition during the planning phase of your capital campaign, as doing so allows you to best budget for such well-deserved recognition. And if you are mid-campaign, take time to regroup and set recognition standards, taking into account gifts received to date.

To create appropriate recognition for your campaign, answer these questions:

1. What form of recognition will be given to each publicized naming gift opportunity — plaques with individual donors' names? A plaque that lists all major donors?
2. Will the various forms of recognition have any degree of consistency even though some will contribute much more than others?
3. How much are we prepared to spend for various forms of donor recognition?
4. Will the recognition given be appropriate for the gift size?
5. Where will each plaque be physically placed?
6. In addition to permanent recognition at our facility, will the donor receive some token of appreciation to display at home or work?
7. Will we want to coordinate a celebration, open house or other event to publicly thank all donors at the campaign's conclusion? How much are we willing to spend for that?
8. Is there a minimum gift amount for which donors will receive special recognition?
9. What process will be followed to ensure donors are selecting the name or names they want included along with proper spelling?

Answers to these and other questions will help ensure donors are appropriately recognized and associated recognition costs are covered.

Identify Ways to Demonstrate Gratitude

This message bears repeating: It is much more cost effective to retain donors than it is to secure new ones. For that reason alone, it's worth the effort to express gratitude to those who have made contributions throughout the year. It's also important to remember that the price of a thank you is much less important than the sincerity of appreciation.

Here are some ways you can express your organization's appreciation to donors throughout the year:

- ❑ Get thank-you letters mailed within 48 hours after a gift has been received.
- ❑ For larger gifts, phone or stop by immediately to express your appreciation. Thank you visits make future solicitation visits more palatable.
- ❑ Use handwritten letters as opposed to typed letters when feasible. They need not be lengthy, but tend to make a communication much more meaningful.
- ❑ Ask those you serve to express appreciation — college students, patients, youth. Those who are served by the generosity of others can best say "thank you."
- ❑ In some cases, give donors a gift that says "thanks." Depending on the size of the gift and the type of nonprofit, recognition gifts can be appropriate. Select gifts that include the name of your organization or your logo — letter openers, paperweights, mugs, plaques, lapel pins. You may even want to consider meaningful gifts that are tied to your organization — art pieces made by college students, bookmarks made by youth, etc. — as a way to express appreciation.
- ❑ Publicly thank donors in your organization's publications. List donors in your newsletter and profile donors and their gifts in feature articles and news releases.
- ❑ Host special events for the benefit of special donors. You may want to consider a once- or twice-a-year reception for those contributing at a certain level.

Bringing the Campaign to a Successful Close

Mark Construction Milestone With Topping-off Ceremony

Is your major construction project stuck between the excitement of a groundbreaking ceremony and the euphoria of a ribbon-cutting ceremony? Why not build up good will and acknowledge key stakeholders with a mid-construction topping-off ceremony?

"A topping-off ceremony is a celebration of the progress made toward completing the construction of a facility," says Gary Friedman, senior associate athletic director at the University of Louisville (Louisville, KY), which recently held a ceremony commemorating progress on a new sports arena.

A topping-off ceremony typically marks the placement of the last or highest beam of a facility's supporting structure. Often painted white and signed by key supporters, the beam is lifted into place amid great fanfare and celebration.

The University of Louisville's star-studded event featured speeches by the chairman of the project's arena authority, university president, athletic director, mayor of Louisville and governor of Kentucky. The 500-plus guests included board members from the arena, university and city, major donors, supporters and purchasers of premium seats.

The event included light hors d'oeuvres, souvenir hardhats and goggles for guests. While the program itself was not lengthy, Friedman says, it accomplished its goal of recognizing the appropriate people and giving everyone a good feeling about the project.

Source: Gary Friedman, Senior Associate Athletic Director, University of Louisville Athletics Department, Louisville, KY. E-mail: gary.friedman@louisville.edu

---

Consider Outdoor Billboards In Special Instances

Here's something you don't see often: a roadside billboard with the photo or illustration of a major donor along with a caption describing his/her recent gift.

While this sort of recognition is not appropriate for every donor, there are instances in which you might want to spotlight a donor's generosity, especially one who relishes that level of publicity and whose level of support merits it.

You might even strike a deal with the outdoor advertiser based on the spirit of the message.

Billboard ads of one or more major donors can send a strong message to people throughout your service region that your organization is worthy of major gifts and make a vivid connection between your charity and respected donors.

Roadside Billboard Ideas

Spotlight principal donors on billboards with an eye-catching photo and caption...

- Thank you, Bruce Duncan, for your exceptional investment in the YMCA!

- Sue Hart ... One in a million! Your generosity will benefit Elgin's youth for generations to come.

- Dallas thanks you, Ace Manufacturing, for investing in the health of our community.

Avoid the Love 'em And Leave 'em Tendency

It's far too common for charities to reach the end of a major campaign only to drastically reduce communication with donors and move on to other things. When that happens, it's a big mistake. People feel unappreciated. Their interest and enthusiasm wanes. And, as you know, there will be a day when you plan to go back to them for another major commitment.

To ensure that current donors get the stewardship they so deserve:

1. Plan a yearlong schedule of inviting donors back to see how their gifts are making an impact on your organization and those served by it.

2. Take steps to see that every major gift includes some form of permanent recognition, depending on its size and type: individual plaques, wall displays that list groups of donors, inclusion in your named endowment literature, etc.

3. Assign others (in addition to yourself) the privilege of calling on select donors to add their words of thanks — board members, other key employees, those served by your organization, etc.

Stewardship Tip

- It's common for those who make major gift commitments to pay off pledges in installments. Each payment represents a great opportunity to not only thank the donor in a personal way, but also to provide updates on how the gift is being used or share the uniqueness of its impact.

Successful Capital Campaigns: From Start to Finish — 3rd Edition

Bringing the Campaign to a Successful Close

Seek Donor Direction When Publicizing Momentous Gifts

When promoting a major gift, structure gift announcements according to donor specifications, says Wendy Walker Zeller, director of donor relations and communications for Washburn Endowment Association, the fundraising arm of Washburn University (Topeka, KS). By properly publicizing major gifts with your donor's wishes in mind, you are letting the donor know how important his/her gift is while increasing the possibility of the donor making another gift to your organization at a later date, says Zeller.

"What the donor wants is foremost in our minds," Zeller says. "If they are unsure, we offer suggestions based on the intention of the gift — where they are making the gift, etc."

Make the gift announcement event pleasing and rewarding for the donor by meeting his/her needs and expectations, says Zeller. Washburn staff work directly with donors to create the experience the donors would like to have at the gift announcement, she says. If a donor will not be present for the announcement, she says, they ask for the donor's input and then share the details of the plan with the donor.

"We try to make the experience a good one for the media as well, keeping in mind the best time of day and most comfortable location to hold a press conference," she says, "ensuring we have adequate lighting and sound and giving access to the donor for questions (if the donor is present and willing)."

When possible, says Zeller, they also prepare a press packet for the media that contains background information for the story.

News releases announcing major gifts are sent to a broad media list, including media outlets that reflect the donor's personal history such as the donor's hometown and the town where his/her employer is headquartered.

Source: Wendy Walker Zeller, Director of Donor Relations & Communications, Washburn Endowment Association, Topeka, KS. E-mail: wwalker@wea.org

Create Policy for Publicizing Momentous Gifts

Take inspiration from these two organizations to publicize your next major gift:

Share Announcement With Those Who Will Benefit From It Most

Washburn University (Topeka, KS) recently received its largest single gift from an individual — a $5 million gift from Trish and Richard Davidson to supplement faculty salaries in its School of Business.

To publicize the momentous gift, Washburn officials turned to the university policy that calls for all gift announcements to be structured to the donor's specifications, says Wendy Walker Zeller, director of donor relations and communications for the Washburn Endowment Association, Washburn University's fundraising arm.

The Davidsons wanted to be present for this gift announcement, Zeller says, "so we spent a great deal of time working out the details to meet their wishes." The Davidsons asked to speak to a class of business students. Also attending the class? The news media, along with the university president, endowment association president, business school dean and board of regents chair. The 100-some students were invited to stay for the gift announcement, which took place just after the press arrived in the classroom.

Media received press packets featuring the Davidsons' biography and were seated at the front of the classroom. A backdrop with the university logo and drape displaying the business school were arranged for the announcement.

Following the gift announcement, says Zeller, the media were invited to interview the donors in a separate location against a backdrop of the university logo.

"Other than a few people on campus and several trustees, we kept the gift amount and identity of the donors under wraps until the official announcement, which helped build suspense and pique press interest," she says. She plans to include an article about the gift in the endowment's annual report and the next issue of the alumni magazine.

Carefully Time Release of News to Maximize Publicity, Impact

Chatham Hall (Chatham, VA), an independent college preparatory high school for girls, recently received a $31 million gift from the estate of Elizabeth Beckwith Nilsen, a former student. The gift was the largest single gift to any girls' independent school.

Because of the magnitude of the gift, Melissa Evans Fountain, director of the office of advancement, says they followed this special plan of action in publicizing it:

On announcement day, classes were delayed until 9:30 a.m. From 8 to 9 a.m., the president of the board and head of school announced the gift to the faculty and answered questions about the gift. At 9 a.m., faculty were joined by the staff and students, and the head of school and board president announced the gift to this larger group.

Staff sent a news release at 9:15 a.m. through US 1 Premium Newswire, the Philanthropy Microlist and the Education Microlist and posted it on the school's website.

At 9:30 a.m., after the all-school meeting, the head of Chatham Hall sent an e-mail announcing the gift to all major educational associations, suggesting they share the news with their constituents.

From 9:30 to 10:30 a.m., calls were made to members of the Alumnae Council and Parent Advisory Council, past heads of the school, certain major donors and other VIPs (all trustees and several top donors knew about the gift prior to the announcement).

At 10:30 a.m. an e-mail blast was sent to all constituents in the school's database and the announcement was posted on the school's Facebook page.

That day, college officials mailed a press release to donor prospects (alumnae, parents and friends) with a cover letter announcing the gift in the context of the school's capital campaign. They also sent the press release to state and local VIPs, area leaders in the Episcopal Church (with which the college is affiliated) and an admission office list that included prospective students and educational consultants. A special article was also written for the school's fall 2009 alumnae magazine.

Sources: Melissa Evans Fountain, Director of the Office of Advancement, Chatham Hall, Chatham, VA. E-mail: mfountain@chathamhall.org
Wendy Walker Zeller, Director of Donor Relations & Communications, Washburn Endowment Association, Topeka, KS. E-mail: wwalker@wea.org

Campaign Evaluation Requires More Than Whether the Goal Was Met

The completion of any capital campaign should include a thorough evaluation that goes far beyond whether or not the campaign goal was met. The results of an evaluation should answer the following questions:

- What was the largest gift contributed?
- What percentage of gifts came from the top 10 to 20 percent of donors?
- How many donors contributed to the campaign overall?
- Which opportunities were most/least popular among donors?
- How many first-time commitments were there?
- What percentage of donors pledged the amount they were asked to give? What percentage gave less than what was asked of them?
- Of total contributions, what percentage was committed by board members?

- What were the percentage contributions of each type?
- What amounts and percentages of gifts came from particular solicitation methods?
- How many volunteers were actively involved?
- What was the campaign budget and how much was it over or under spent?
- What percentage of gifts came from each campaign phase?
- How did the campaign consultant meet, exceed or fail to meet expectations?
- How did staff meet, exceed or fail to meet expectations?
- What external factors (e.g., local economy, competition for philanthropic support, etc.) impacted the campaign?
- What internal factors (e.g., staff proficiency, budget, etc.) impacted the campaign?

Campaign Ending? Forget the Gala

Ball State University's (Muncie, IN) Ball State Bold campaign raised $210 million from more than 65,000 donors over a number of years. But where many would commemorate the end of such an endeavor with a grand celebration, university officials did the exact opposite, scrapping the gala altogether.

"More organizations are moving in that direction, I think" says Kelly Shrock, associate executive director of development. "Lavish celebrations can give the appearance of being unwise with the funds you've raised, and that can be frustrating to donors. So you really want to be careful about the extent that you celebrate."

Instead of throwing such a fete, campaign organizers established the Bold Celebration scholarship program. "It was something that we promoted in all our campaign materials — the idea that in lieu of a glitzy campaign wrap-up we were offering an opportunity to celebrate by supporting students," says Shrock. She notes that officials had hoped to create 25 scholarships but ended up receiving enough support to fund 55. "It's was a message that was very well received."

The initiative's impact was further leveraged by showcasing Bold Celebration scholars at a number of regional wrap-up events. "It was sort of a campaign victory tour," explains Schrock. "It gave donors a chance to hear students' own words about how the campaign scholarships made their education possible."

These events are still ongoing over a half-year past the campaign's official close. In fact, organizers made a point of decoupling the campaign's formal end from its celebration and commemoration. "Day-of" publicity events included a banner announcement on the university's website and a press release, but other print ads, feature articles and billboards were saved for release at strategic points later in the year.

The ceremonial announcement of the end of the campaign was similarly delayed, allowing it to piggyback with a previously scheduled recognition event. "We didn't try to cram everything into the week of the close" Shrock says. "July is not the preferred month for our constituency, so we saved a lot of things for the 'fall drumbeat.'"

Shrock says organizers began making end-of-campaign plans about 20 months before the close date. For organizations approaching the end of a first campaign, she suggests convening a meeting three to six months out to decide what metrics and statistics will be most important in telling the story of the campaign. "It allows you to start gathering preliminary information in the areas you're interested in. That way, when the campaign actually closes, you can quickly produce the reports you need."

Source: Kelly Shrock, Associate Executive Director of Development, Ball State University, Muncie, IN. E-mail: Kkshrock@bsu.edu

---

What About Internal Celebrations?

Officials at Ball State University (Muncie, IN) declined to mark the end of their Ball State Bold campaign with large celebrations for donors or supporters. But that doesn't mean internal staff didn't get a little bash of their own.

"When we hit the publicized goal, we had a champagne and sparkling-grape juice toast in the development office," says Kelly Shrock, associate executive director of development. "The announcement came when the foundation's board of directors was in town, so a lot of volunteers were able to take part in the celebration, as well."

But Shrock says thanking other internal departments is also crucial. "We're always thinking about thanking donors, but we need to also help internal partners understand how important they are to a campaign's success."

Accordingly, Shrock and several other development staff bought doughnuts at a local bakery and delivered boxes to four key offices. "We pasted a picture on the top of each box and all wrote notes of thanks on it when the campaign was over. We also had someone taking pictures of the shocked faces we saw, and later put together a scrap book to pass around. It was all very genuine and collaborative."

Such efforts are important for the long-term health of an organization, says Schrock. "It's all too easy to ignore the people we work with on a day-to-day basis."

Successful Capital Campaigns: From Start to Finish, Third Edition.
Edited by Scott C. Stevenson.
© 2012 Stevenson, Inc. Published 2012 by Stevenson, Inc.

Successful Capital Campaigns: From Start to Finish — 3rd Edition

Capital Campaign Case Studies

Many of our capital campaign successes are learned from what others have done correctly and, in some cases, failed to do correctly. Learn from this small sampling of capital campaign case studies and success stories to discover what might be applied to your own fundraising endeavors.

How to Get Your First Major Capital Campaign Off the Ground

Southern Illinois University Edwardsville (Edwardsville, IL) was a young university with an evolving development program. But with a 50th anniversary on the horizon, the transition to Division I athletics, a recent change in university leadership and a cut in state funding, officials knew the time was right to launch the institution's first capital campaign.

The university launched the public portion of its capital campaign in March 2011 with $26 million already in hand.

Patrick Hundley, vice chancellor for university relations and executive director of the Southern Illinois University Edwardsville Foundation, answers questions about the $50 million Defining Excellence campaign and the process of starting a first major gifts campaign:

What did the university do to prepare for the capital campaign?

"We started by hiring a consultant to undertake a feasibility study and help us prepare a communications plan. We brought in a professional fundraiser to give a one-day fundraising workshop for the deans of our nine academic units. And we also formed a campaign steering committee to coordinate everything."

What new or different tools did you use in launching the campaign?

"Sending a list of alumni to a wealth screening service was very helpful. It allowed us to find people of capacity whom we weren't aware of, and has provided years' worth of prospects."

What challenges did you encounter shifting from annual fundraising to a capital campaign?

"The biggest issue was a lack of emphasis on major gifts. Our development officers weren't used to going after six-figure gifts, so we had to teach people how to ask for big gifts in addition to small ones. We also did training on how to write proposals for big gifts."

Did the structure of your fundraising operation need to be changed?

"Over the years, our fundraisers picked up a lot of duties with things like the annual report, golf tournament and honors dinner, so asking them to go see 75 top donors as well created time-management challenges. We are currently hiring for several new positions."

What advice do you have for other institutions starting a first capital campaign?

- "Have a consultant do a feasibility study before you start, especially the first time out, because you have to make sure you have a solid constituency of people who can not only make big gifts, but also introduce you to other people who can also make big gifts."

- "I highly recommend a wealth screening type of prospecting service, particularly for a group that doesn't already have a large major gifts prospect pool."

- "Budget plenty of travel money. You don't want to let the fact that a prospect is out in California stop you from reaching out in the most effective way possible."

- "In setting a first campaign goal, it's much better to exceed your goal than to kill yourself trying to make a stretch goal. If your feasibility study says $25 million is possible, you might want to consider aiming for $20 million or $23 million."

Source: Patrick Hundley, Vice Chancellor for University Relations and Executive Director, SIUE Foundation, Southern Illinois University Edwardsville, Edwardsville, IL. E-mail: phundle@siue.edu

Reach Out to Supportive Families With a Children's Wall

Capital campaigns are always in need of creative funding strategies, particularly at mid levels of donation. Approaches that generate ongoing relationships (as opposed to just one-time gifts) are similarly sought after.

To accomplish both goals, consider a major gift project that reaches out to entire families, including young children.

Officials at the Kauffman Center for the Performing Arts (Kansas City, MO) established just this kind of outreach with their Children's Wall, a donor recognition project that allows children, grandchildren or other young friends of donors to leave their handprint on a specially designated section of the under-construction facility.

When completed, the project will feature 1,000 handprints arranged along the approach to the center's main lobby. Each entry will include the name of the child being honored and year the handprint was created. (Handprints can be captured and submitted remotely, ensuring appeal to supporters beyond the immediate Kansas City area.)

For $1,000 per handprint, donors can give a youngster special to them a one-of-a-kind experience, and center officials can begin building connections with a new generation of potential supporters.

Source: Kauffman Center for the Performing Arts, Kansas City, MO. E-mail: contact@kauffmancenter.org

Set Goals to Exceed Feasibility Study Expectations

Even with all the fundraising technology, trends and techniques available today, a major capital campaign's success still comes down to the most crucial component of all: people passionate about a cause.

That passion helped Chesapeake Service Systems (Chesapeake, VA) greatly exceed a feasibility study's predictions for a recent campaign.

In June 2005, the nonprofit organization that finds employment for adults with mental retardation, autism and other severe disabilities expanded its laundry occupational center, providing employment for 200-plus persons. Prior to the facility's opening, a well-respected consulting firm conducted a feasibility study and concluded that the group would only raise a few hundred thousand dollars for the project at best.

So how did Tom Swanston, Chesapeake's executive director, wind up raising close to $5 million for the organization's capital campaign, almost single-handedly?

"You must set a goal, first and foremost," Swanston says. "Second, you must believe in that goal. Third, you must have a good case for support. Fourth, the leader of the campaign must decide that the goal will happen."

Armed with the courage of your convictions, Swanston says, put to use these subtle communication strategies that lead to success:

✓ Before submitting a proposal, contact a potential donor in person if possible, or at least by phone. This way, you do not waste their time or yours. Swanston backs up this tip with statistics from his experiences: "Our success rate is approximately 10 percent on a cold proposal, 40 percent on a proposal where there was a call first, 75 percent on a proposal with face-to-face contact and 90 percent when they see the operation."

✓ Establish relationships and be intelligently passionate, says Swanston, reiterating the time-proven axiom: "People ultimately give to people."

✓ Keep following up until you get an answer. "Understand that the only bad answer is the lack of an answer," he says. "If someone tells me no, I consider that a success because I have persisted and gotten an answer."

✓ List other donors in your proposal. They are your references.

✓ Don't ask for what you want. Ask for what the donor wants to give you.

✓ Take a vested interest in your donor's success, he says: "Make them feel like they are champions."

✓ Let every donor know that his or her gift is working in concert with copious other givers to achieve something big.

✓ Say thank you, have the board say thank you and find abundant, different ways to say thank you.

✓ Communicate abundantly with your donors even when you are not making an ask. Share information and updates, and touch base with them as the project evolves, so they know what their money is accomplishing.

Source: Tom Swanston, Executive Director, Chesapeake Service Systems, Chesapeake, VA. E-mail: info@css-online.com

Despite Economic Downturn, Campaign Transcends Boundaries

What does it mean when the perfect storm of circumstances indicate that you should extend your campaign by two years and increase your goal not just once, but twice? You do it, of course! At least that's what happened with Goucher College's (Baltimore, MD) capital campaign, Transcending Boundaries, The Campaign for Goucher College.

"The economy was good, donors were generous, and the college received a number of unexpected generous bequests," says Vice President for Development and Alumnae/i Affairs Janet Wiley.

"In August of 2008, the president and the campaign executive committee predicted that we would reach our goal one full year ahead of schedule, coinciding with the opening of a brand new 125,000 square foot facility, the Athenaeum, and the beginning of the college's 125th year. In many ways, it was the perfect storm — momentum was calling," she says.

In September 2009, at the opening of the Athenaeum, and the launch of the 125th year celebration, the committee announced that the campaign goal had been met, and that they were forging forward to $100 million and extending the campaign for two additional years.

Unfortunately, one month later, the bottom dropped out of the economy. Still, feedback was mostly positive, and the president, volunteers and staff continued to push hard, extending campaign commitments from loyal donors and attempting to find and develop new donors at record speed.

In order to make that happen, says Wiley, the college converted to a new development database — a move that had been delayed due to the disruption that a year-long conversion would cause in the campaign. That, and a $3 million challenge grant from the state of Maryland, have helped the school meet and exceed all expectations.

"We have truly 'transcended boundaries,'" says Wiley. "We are six months into our database conversion and are on track to meet the $3M challenge grant from the state. And we are uncovering new donor prospects at the speed of light. We have three new endowed chairs, a new environmental science major and the college continues to be on solid financial ground."

The campaign will officially conclude on June 30, 2012, with campaign totals currently nearing $106 million. Wiley says by the end of the campaign they hope to be well into the renovation of the new academic center, in concert with the new strategic plan.

Source: Janet Wiley, Vice President for Development and Alumnae/i Affairs, Goucher College, Baltimore, MD.
E-mail: janet.wiley@goucher.edu

College Conducts Successful Two-phase Campaign

Development officials at Ivy Tech Community College, Southern Indiana (Sellersburg, IN) decided to divide its multimillion dollar capital campaign, Changing Lives. Building Futures, into two phases.

They did so for several reasons, says Andrew Takami, executive director of development, including the need to be sensitive to the nature of the economy in their community and the fact that it was their first-ever capital campaign.

According to Takami, their campaign consultant also recommended, based on a feasibility study, that the college could raise $3-4 million, while college officials had initially thought they could raise only $1.5 million.

"By starting with a smaller phase one goal, we aimed to achieve early success and keep everyone excited and motivated to move on to the next phase," says Takami.

The plan worked. Four months into the first phase of the campaign, they had exceeded their phase one goal of $2 million by $200,000. Seven months into the second phase of the campaign, the college had raised $2.7 million.

Takami says they have not announced an overall campaign goal and have set no end date for the campaign, although the active solicitation portion will last 16 months.

He adds that they initially wanted to fundraise only to support components of the new building for which the Indiana General Assembly had allocated $20 million.

"The consultant recommended we provide donors with an opportunity to support more than one initiative, so we decided to include options to support student scholarships and department-specific programs, such as endowed chairs," he says.

The capital campaign will also launch an external, comprehensive annual campaign — the college's first-ever continual annual fund.

The key to the success of a phased campaign, says Takami, is keeping campaign volunteer committee members motivated and engaged. One way they are accomplishing that is through their committee structure, which has an executive committee and four subcommittees. The executive committee is chaired by the co-campaign chairs and includes the four subcommittee chairs and the college's CFOs, marketing directors and other internal staff. There are also other key community leaders on the committee.

"The subcommittees are set up so that when their work is done, their committee is disbanded," he says. "For example, one of the committees was a prospect research committee. They researched the prospects and then gave their research to the lead gifts committee and advance gifts committee. The prospect research committee was then disbanded.

"This structure helps energize committee members," Takami says, "because they can clearly see their mission and when the commission of their work is over, they are done."

Source: Andrew Takami, Executive Director of Development, Ivy Tech Community College, Southern Indiana, Sellersburg, IN. E-mail: atakami@ivytech.edu